Blessed Broken & Given

By

Dr. Elaine Shouse Waller

ISBN 979-8-89480-463-7

Written by Dr. Elaine Shouse Waller

Edited by Leeds Press Corp, Staff.

Leedspublishing.com

Twitter.com/leedspresscorp

Instagram.com/leedspresscorp

Facebook.com/leedspresscorp

Printed in the United States of America

Table of Contents

To my son, Jerome Waller, III,
"thank you" for always inspiring me
to speak the truth in love.

To Jerome Waller, Jr.,
"thank you" for consistently.
being a C.E.O (Chief Encouraging Officer)
insisting that I have something valuable
to share with others.
Your push has been valuable to me.

And to my sister, friend
and co-laborer in Ministry, Rebecca G. Lay;
"thank you" for your patience in the original typing –
I am sincerely grateful!

Introduction

"I Grew Up In Sunday School"

Growing up in a Pentecostal-Holiness family allowed me to be persuaded that I knew three things about God. They were always clearly like "stage-center" in my mind: First, I knew that God is good; secondly, I knew that God said He loved me and would never leave me; and thirdly, I knew that God is sovereign, and He always knows what He is doing! These three convictions about the character of God have always given me faith to hold onto in times of trouble and even in times of confusion and uncertainty. In most of the important decisions and choices in my life – these three principles, I believed about God, have persuaded me to run to Him for help in times of trouble, and He would always be there!

My father, was a man who sought and taught "great faith." It was my opinion, during my younger years, that Dad was too dogmatic about faith in God. However, his lifestyle and convictions taught me that God develops faith and character through our human sufferings. I still believe this principle is a Christian principle of truth and one that Spirit-based faith walkers should use as a spiritual perspective. Why? Because it has taught me to walk humbly before God, yet not allow others to interpret God and what He wants out of my life. It has taught me to go directly to the Word of God – the scripture; and to follow the leading of the Holy Ghost! My eleven sisters and three brothers were all taught this principle.

The next greatest, spiritual influence in my life was that I grew up in Sunday School! Yes, I am certain that what I learned about God, Jesus as my Lord, and Savior, and living a new life in Christ was developed in me through Sunday School classes. I truly loved going to Sunday School. Now, that I think about it, as a little girl around the age of five, my weekly excitement was attending the "Beginner's Class" at Calvary Missionary Baptist Church in Terre Haute, Indiana. Right before I turned twelve years, my father had experienced the baptism of the Holy Ghost and moved our family to assemble with a Pentecostal-Holiness Church – True Gospel Tabernacle. True Gospel was a one hundred percent Apostolic-Holiness Church. For me, the best thing about this spiritual transition was Sunday School. I will always remember that Mother (who had also just received the new-birth experience – baptism of the Holy Ghost) told me that "now that we are a Pentecostal, Sunday School classes will help us become 'transformed' to a Christ-like character." That was a good enough explanation for me. Then, the first Sunday School teacher that I had in this Pentecostal environment said that 'transformation' means 'an inside change of heart and character.' That settled my thinking! I wanted to learn and really experience this knowledge and power that could only come from the Bible and be imparted to me through the Holy Ghost using my teachers. Yes, it created in me a desire, a hunger to be taught the knowledge of the Word of God. By the time I turned thirteen I believed that God was always doing something new in my life. So, I tried to be open-minded when I encountered truth that I had not heard nor seen – or even imagined. I truly grew to love being taught the true stories and knowledge of the scriptures.

It is still quite exciting to reflect on the early years of my encounters with God through the simplicity of Sunday School lessons. I hope that you can feel the joy and peace that is in my soul and spirit as I share with you! Today, I hope that you too have learned as much about God's peace and joy you can experience when you allow Him to be in charge of your life. Today, I hope that you too, will grasp the peace and assurance that only God offers us in a hard, complex, and conflicting society. I offer you these few pages in the assurance that there is hope in your future if Jesus is in the center of your present experience. In the next pages of the book, I hope to encourage you in knowing that trusting God and making His will for your life your greatest desire. I learned at a very early age that putting God in second place will never do. I was told by a Sunday School teacher: "If God is not your first priority, you may-as-well take Him off your list!" Making the Kingdom of God your primary concern means that you will prioritize your life around God and His will for your life.

Stop for a moment and think about it: God is the Designer, Creator and Sustainer of all life. With these credentials, shouldn't you and I trust Him with the decisions about our lives? John's gospel presents Jesus as:

The True Shepherd

"But he who enters by the door is the shepherd of the sheep." ***(John 10:2)***

The Good Shepherd

"I am the good shepherd. The good shepherd gives His life for the sheep." ***(John 10:11)***

The Shepherd That Knows His Sheep

"I am the good shepherd; and I know My sheep and am known by My own." ***(John 10:14)***

"My sheep hear My voice, and I know them, and they follow Me." ***(John 10:27)***

My aim in this book is to first, affirm your trust in God and strengthen your confidence in the reality that God is with you and will never, never, never abandon you! Secondly, I share some faith principles I have learned through my own trials and struggles. These principles have taught me how to interpret God's purpose while going through what seems to be bad circumstances. Knowing and applying God's Word appropriately will build a faith in you that chooses to believe God's Word above all the feelings of human emotions. Yes, you too can build your faith in God's Word. A faith that does not deny the difficulty of circumstances; rather a dogmatic and resilient faith which trust fully in God's Word and makes decisions that are in agreement with it!

The third goal of this book is to share with you a pattern that God has taught me through the scripture and life experiences with Him. I have observed this pattern when I have been in circumstances that have made me ask: "Where is God in this" and "What does He want me to do?" These questions, I believe, seem to dominate our ability to interpret what God is doing in us, through us and with us. I am persuaded that as we walk with God's guidance through the testing, developing, and building of our faith, He will show us that He is always blessing us; breaking our resistance and human will; and then giving us for service to others for His glory in the earth! Therefore, I title these experiences and lessons – **Blessed, Broken and Given**.

Beloved of God, as you read, be assured that trusting God for your future, really does began with trusting God now! It is true, that once you have committed yourself to doing God's will (regardless of what it cost you), God will be with you and guide you. The Apostle Paul says it better:

"...being confident of this very thing, that He who has begun a good work in you will complete it until the day of Jesus Christ;" ***(Philippians 1:6).***

Lesson One

Asking the Right Questions

I spiritually and literally grew up in Sunday School. I was taught the scriptures. Through good Sunday-School teachers, whom I loved, I was taught to hold onto every word and moment of learning! It was in the "Intermediate Class" (that's the Middle School age class) when I knew that I was "called" to be a teacher and I would passionately pursue every level of preparation for fulfilling that desire. The second major influence which Sunday School had upon me was that – constructive, healthy learning involves developing the ability to ask the right questions. I have been involved in higher education all my adult life and I have utilized this principle. I have consistently taught others that "evidence of effective learning is when the student has learned to ask the right question."

In these troubled and end-times that we live in today, I believe that born-again Christians must have the spiritual maturity to look at life situations and ask God and themselves the right questions. Recently, I heard a national political leader say, "I am so greatly disturbed and confused with the situation of our political culture – that I don't even know what questions to address." This kind of confusion clearly suggests that this person has no solid core beliefs. Even the young, new-born Christian with me responded and immediately quoted **Romans 8:28**: *"And we know that* *all things work together for good for those who love God and are the called according to His purpose."*

Certainly, those of us who are what Apostle Paul calls "new creatures in Christ" who have allowed our life purpose to be defined by the will and purposes of God can be encouraged with Romans 8:28. Daily, we have the godly privilege to conclusively say that "whatever happens to us – God will bring good out of it." I saw a bumper sticker on an automobile that read: "Nothing Bad Can Happen to Me »**Romans 8:28**." My response was a smile and then – Amen!

However, it is imperative that you be reminded that you need to have the spiritual maturity to look at your questionable life situations and ask God the right questions! I have found the story and details of God's use of Gideon to provide for us an excellent illustration and method of how to respond to God in difficult times. Yes, God often allows life circumstances to hit and impact us in such a way that we must ask, "What is this about?" Often, we will have to turn to God because we can't interpret where He is in the situation. Sometimes, the things are so bad...so evil in the details, that you find it hard to believe that God is in it; or that God is still with you.

Judges, chapter 6, 7 and 8 present us with the story of God in Gideon's affairs. It is worth your time to read all three of the chapters. However, I will focus on chapter 6, because by itself you will see the perspective you need – as God chooses to work in your lives:

Judges 6:11-18 – 11; *Now the Angel of the Lord came and sat under the terebinth tree, which was in Ophrah, which belonged to Joash the Abiezrite, while his son Gideon threshed wheat in the winepress, in order to hide it from the Midianites.*
12 And the Angel of the Lord appeared to him, and said to him, "The Lord is with you, you mighty man of valor!" 13 Gideon
said to Him, "O my lord, if the Lord is with us, why then has all this happened to us? And where are all His miracles which our fathers told us about, saying, 'Did not the Lord bring us up from Egypt?' But now the Lord has forsaken us and delivered us into the hands of the Midianites." 14 Then the Lord turned
to him and said, "Go in this might of yours, and you shall save Israel from the hand of the Midianites. Have I not sent you?"
15 So he said to Him, "O my Lord, how can I save Israel? Indeed, my clan is the weakest in Manasseh, and I am the least
in my father's house." 16 And the Lord said to him, "Surely I will be with you, and you shall defeat the Midianites as one
man." 17 Then he said to Him, "If now I have found favor in Your sight, then show me a sign that it is You who talk with
me. 18 Do not depart from here, I pray, until I come to You and bring out my offering and set it before You." And He said, "I will wait until you come back."

I see in this sixth chapter a significant model for us today, as we struggle to interpret God in our affairs.

Let's look at this:

Point #1 (verse 11) – When the angel shows up to give Gideon his assignment; Gideon is threshing wheat in the winepress, hiding from the Midianites.

- Normally, wheat was threshed in an open space that would catch a breeze of open wind so that chaff was blown away.

Point #**2** (verse 12) – The Angel of the Lord said to Gideon, *"The Lord is with you, you mighty man of valor!"*

Point #**3** (Verse 13) – Gideon's response is the KEY to my application: Gideon asked two significant questions in verse 13:

Two Key Questions:

Why is this happening?

Where is God in this?

↣ Gideon said to Him, *"O my lord, if the Lord is with us, why then has all this happened to us...?"*

I know that many preachers and theologians have focused on the fact that Gideon was afraid and hiding. Well, wouldn't you be? The Midianites were said to be like a great swarm of locusts. They stole or destroyed everything in their sight. **Chapter 6,** verses 2-5: *2 and the hand of Midian prevailed against Israel. Because of the Midianites, the children of Israel made for themselves the dens, the caves, and the strongholds which are in the mountains. 3 So it was, whenever Israel had sown, Midianites would come up; also, Amalekites and the people of the East would come up against them. 4 Then they would encamp against them and destroy the produce of the earth as far as Gaza, and leave no sustenance for Israel, neither sheep nor ox nor donkey. 5 For they would* *come up with their livestock and their tents, coming in as numerous as locusts; both they and their camels were without number; and they would enter the land to destroy it.*

You must pay attention to the detail given, to clearly display that the Midianites and the Amalekites were coming into Israel's land to steal and destroy it. Israel had become poverty-stricken and had begun to cry out to the Lord. In view of their present circumstances, God had forsaken them. Sadly enough, Gideon asked much like we still do today, the "why" question. At the top of chapter 6, we are given the reason why. Why? Israel had forgotten how God had delivered them of the oppression of Egypt and all others who had oppressed them. God had also sent a prophet to the Children of Israel to remind them they had become disobedient and would suffer the consequences. Yet, the Children of Israel chose to disobey God. So, the reason they were suffering was because they had violated the Covenant they had with God – Yes, they were suffering the consequences. Doesn't these issues of disobedience sound familiar?

However, take notice that God heard their cry and responds by sending an angel. Surprisingly, while Gideon is going to great lengths to hide from the Midianites, God sends His messenger to Gideon's hiding place and actually commissioned Gideon to deliver the Children of Israel from their enemies:

"And the Angel of the Lord appeared to him, and said to him, "The Lord is with you, you mighty man of valor!" (verse 12)

- And, although Gideon could only see from his own circumstances and not the big picture – God's plan, the angel says to him the answer to Gideon's question #2:

"Where is God in this?

Point #4 (verse 14) – God gives Gideon his assignment!

"Then the Lord turned to him and said, "Go in this might of yours, and you shall save Israel from the hand of the Midianites. Have I not sent you."

Gideon, still looking from his limited small perspective responds with his disclaimer saying: *"O my Lord, how can I save Israel?"* (verse 15). The Lord says to Gideon what He is still saying to us today:

Point #5 (verse 16) – I will be with you!

And the Lord said to him, "Surely I will be with you, and you shall defeat the Midianites as one man."

Gideon's success was dependent on whether the Lord was in the situation. It required that the Lord declare "I am with you!" Do you get it! Are you asking the two questions that Gideon asked when the struggle was about to overtake him?

Why is this happening?

Where is God in this?

When you humbly go to God and ask these two questions, I know that He will answer and show you the path that He has already prepared for you. Remember, this is the same God who said to us, *'Call to Me, and I will answer you, and show you great and mighty things, which you do not know'* ***(Jeremiah 33:3).***

You are not only a part of God's plan, but you are valuable to God's plan! God tells us through **Jeremiah 29:11**, *"For I know the thoughts that I think toward you, says the Lord, thoughts of peace and not of evil, to give you a future and a hope."* This event in the book of Judges that focuses on Gideon, emphasizes the necessity of trusting God's presence and His divine resources, rather than your own. Before Gideon's story ends, we learn that the Midianites were shattered by the power of God working through the people of God – even in the midst of dark circumstances. Look at this closely – God, used Gideon without any military weapons. Gideon's untrained men were placed into three groups: (1) men with clap pitchers; (2) men with torches; and (3) men with trumpets. Remember, the angel (who was also referred to as the "Lord" – verse 14), said to Gideon, "*Surely I will be with you, and you shall defeat the Midianites as one man*" (verse 16). Your task is to do the assignments that God has given you, while understanding that you too are walking in the presence of God! God responded to Gideon's feelings of inadequacy, just as He did with Moses' concerns – "*I will be with you!*" We must believe that God strengthens those He calls and commissions. Trust in the promise of His abiding presence.

In these times we live, it is important that we gain faith principles from the events of Gideon and know this: Even when we don't understand things and think that the odds are against us; God calls us to do great things -great works. Yes, but great works are only done His way; and learn to ask God the right questions. Then, trust Him and wait for His instructions. Gideon also demonstrated some valuable traits of godly relationship which we would be wise to immolate:

- Willingness to turn faith into action (**Judges 6:25-27; 7:15-22).**
- Unwilling to lead unless God calls and instructs **(6:36-42).**
- Dependence on God for every turn and every decision **(7:1-8).**
- He and the people gave glory to God before and after each victory **(7:15; 8:3, 23; 8:6).**
- His willingness to use the gifts God had given him to lead others.

*Take notice that he told the 300 who remained (stuck it out!) with him to observe his example (7:17).

Lastly, it is important for our interest in character development to take notice that Gideon refused to establish a "self-dynasty" after God, and he had fulfilled his God assignment (see chapter 8:22-23).

The next five chapters of this book are intended to help you examine the biblical principles that will assist you and help you to have a clearer understanding of how God's divine purposes are most often fulfilled in our lives. Also, these principles will help to stop your misinterpreting where God is in your difficult and seemingly – unrighteous circumstances of life. I have learned, and so will you, that life has a way of slapping you with some painful and confusing events, which can leave you spinning and asking "Where is God? And "Why is this happening?" During the COVID-19 Pandemic, a great number of Christians found themselves overwhelmed with more questions than answers. Many believers are still asking, "What's next? I don't know?" see or hear Jesus in the midst of trouble, it's because you don't have Him in the highest place of your perspective! The enemy of your soul wants your thinking to become so flawed that it damages your perspective of God. So, do not make the mistake of thinking that God has abandoned you when hardship or trouble enters your life. God has not abandoned you in these things and His presence is still with you. You can be sure that God is there and wants to reveal Himself to you when you are experiencing difficulties.

The next five chapters of this book will help you learn how to find God in these types of circumstances. We must learn to use difficult circumstances and life's situations, as we learn how God is using them to teach us more about who He is, and how to allow things to be used to serve a beneficial purpose in our lives. Yes, God's divine purpose is at work in your life! You are on His "Assignment in His Kingdom" list. God is with you. He promised to never leave you, nor forsake you. If to take God at His word and expect to find Him in even your darkest hours, you will be joyfully surprised to see His purposes being done!

Lesson Two

Knowing God (And Seeking His Will)

I was in the twelfth grade of high school, about to graduate and turn eighteen years old, when my Sunday School teacher told the class that he needed to tell us an important fact. I remember thinking in that moment, "Oh boy, I'm about to really spiritually grow-up." Then he slowly spoke it: "Satan does not want you to know God's will." Before we could respond, he continued: "The word of God reveals God's will. So, if you don't know His word, you will not know his will and purpose for your life." That class – that day, became a turning point and life-changing event for me. I felt a new level of godly fear and had a real sense of holy reverence for the word of God! That night before I went to bed I told God, in my bed-time prayer, that there were three Scriptures, I needed Him to write on my heart. They were:

Psalm 119:105 *– "Your word is a lamp to my feet and a light to my path."*

Psalm 40:8 *– "I delight to do Your will, O my God, and Your law is within my heart."*

Psalm 27:4 *– "One thing I have desired of the Lord, that will I seek: That I may dwell in the house of the Lord All the days of my life, to behold the beauty of the Lord, and to inquire in His temple."*

Now, I would like to briefly share with you another lesson I learned in Sunday School, when I learned the goal of the devil was to rob me of my knowledge of the "will" of God – I decided I would become a "student of the Word." I took this as a personal threat. I began to understand that if I allowed Satan to accomplish this in my life, it meant that I would never know my purpose. Furthermore, the devil would rob me of my destiny and purpose in the Kingdom of God. Let us remember what Jesus said: "*The thief does not come except to steal, and to kill, and to destroy*";

I have come that they may have life, and that they may have it more abundantly" ***(John 10:10)***.

Clearly, the word of God – the Bible, (the written Word) is the major source for all who believe, to have access to the will of God for their lives. First, we know that the will of God is the true expression of God's love toward us. King David comprehended and released the profound beauty of this truth in Psalm 139. David speaks of God's perfect knowledge and loving purpose of mankind: *3 "You comprehend my path and my lying down and are acquainted with all my ways. 4 For there is not a word on my tongue, but behold, O Lord, You know it altogether. 5 You have hedged me behind and before and laid Your hand upon me. Such knowledge is too wonderful for me; It is high, I cannot attain it."* ***(Psalm 139:3-6)***.

The palmist continues and speaks of the omnipotence and omnipresent character of the Creator:

"14 I will praise You, for I am fearfully and wonderfully made; Marvelous are Your works, and that my soul knows very well. 16 Your eyes saw my substance, being yet unformed. And in Your book, they all were written, The days fashioned for me, When as yet there were none of them. 17 How precious also are Your thoughts to me, O God! How great is the sum of them!" ***(Psalm 139:14, 16-17)****.*

Throughout the Psalms we are told of God's lovingkindness and the truth of His character, that is presented in His Word: 2*"I will worship toward Your holy temple and praise Your name for Your lovingkindness and Your truth; For You have magnified Your word above all Your name. 3 In the day when I cried out, You answered me, and made me bold with strength in my soul." (**Psalm 138:2-3**).* God wants all of us to know His will. *"...'The God of our fathers has chosen you that you should know His will, and see the Just One, and hear the voice of His mouth." (**Acts 22:14**).*

There are three characteristics of God that I have held onto in order to keep a godly perspective about my relationship with God.

They are:

#1 God wants to be known and His Word and Holy Spirit provide that knowledge.

#2 God wants a relationship with us; and-

#3 God wants to be understood!

Let us take a quick look at these three facts that have built my faith and kept me confident about *"knowing God"* and "*seeking His will.*" Yes, the scriptures validate this:

I. God Wants to be Known.

From the beginning, God has wanted to be known by mankind. Even after the fall of Adam and Eve, God's purpose prevailed:

Jeremiah 32:38-41, *38"They shall be My people, and I will be their God; 39 then I will give them one heart and one way, that they may fear Me forever, for the good of them and their children after them. 40 And I will make an everlasting covenant with them, that I will not turn away from doing them good; but I will put My fear in their hearts so that they will not depart from Me. 41 Yes, I will rejoice over them to do them good, and I will assuredly plant them in this land, with all My heart and with all My soul.' 38 They shall be My people, and I will be their God; 39 then I will give them one heart and one way, that they may fear Me forever, for the good of them and their children after them. 40 And I will make an everlasting covenant with them, that I will not turn away from doing them good; but I will put My fear in their hearts so that they will not depart from Me. 41 Yes, I will rejoice over them to do them good, and I will assuredly plant them in this land, with all My heart and with all My soul.'"*

We must understand that God has had His purpose planted within us from the beginning: ***Isaiah 46:9-10 - 9*** *... I am God, and there is no other; I am God, and there is none like Me, 10 Declaring the end from the beginning, and from* *ancient times things that are not yet done, saying, 'My counsel shall stand, and I will do all My pleasure,'*

You are not an experiment: You were born to manifest something divine – the will of God, which has already been finished through the redemptive work of Jesus Christ. This is why you must live by faith; always looking forward with expectation for what God has already planned and completed on your behalf:

Ecclesiastes 3:14-15 - *14 I know that whatever God does, it shall be forever. Nothing can be added to it, and nothing taken from it. God does it, that men should fear before Him.*
15 That which is has already been, and what is to be has already been; And God requires an account of what is past.

Stay persuaded (confident) that God's will and plans for you are good!

Jeremiah 29:11 - *For I know the thoughts that I think toward you, says the Lord, thoughts of peace and not of evil, to give you a future and hope.*

Continuously trust in the truth that God has given you; assurance of open access to Himself:

Jeremiah 33:2-3 - *2 "Thus says the Lord who made it, the Lord who formed it to establish it (the Lord is His name):*
3 'Call to Me, and I will answer you, and show you great and mighty things, which you do not know."

Rejoice that God's gifts and callings are within and they are irrevocable:

Romans 11:29 - *For the gifts and the calling of God are irrevocable.*

Choose to know and believe that the Word of God has been proven to be absolutely Trustworthy. So, now your position is to:

Psalm 37:4 - *Delight yourself also in the Lord, and He shall give you the desires of your heart.*

Get excited! God wants us to know His will. *"The God of our fathers has appointed you to know His will"* ***(Acts 22:14)***. The Apostle Paul also instructs, that God wants us to understand His will when it says in ***Ephesians 5:17:*** *Therefore, do not be unwise, but understand what the will of the Lord is.* Furthermore, Paul says, *"... do not cease to pray for you, and to ask that you may be filled with the knowledge of His will in all wisdom and spiritual understanding;* ***(Colossians 1:9)***.

II. God Wants A Relationship With Us

"For God so loved..." Again, read this most familiar verse in the Bible and take notice of your goosebumps!

"*For God so loved the world that He gave His only begotten Son, that whoever believes in Him should not perish but have everlasting life.* ***(John 3:16)***.

This verse certainly is the theme of the Gospels; it expresses God's love made manifest in an infinitely, glorious manner – Jesus Christ. This verse speaks a fundamental truth of God's character, which we would do well to always remember. God's unconditional love, love by choice and by an act of His will. There is no better way to affirm God's desire for relationship with us, other than the fact that His motivation for "giving" us Jesus – was His love. He gave His only begotten Son. God gave His very best.

Take notice of these key factors of truth:

God gave sacrificially...
Isaiah 53:4-5 - 4 *Surely, He has borne our griefs and carried our sorrows; Yet we esteemed Him stricken, smitten by God, and afflicted.* [5] *But He was wounded for our transgressions, He was bruised for our iniquities; The chastisement for our peace was upon Him, and by His stripes we are healed.*

Salvation through Jesus Christ gives us a relationship with God, wherein we are completely and continually accepted because of our position in Christ. With revelation and joy, we hold onto the words of ***2 Corinthians 5:17-19, 21:*** *17 Therefore, if anyone is in Christ, he is a new creation; old things have passed away; behold, all things have become new. 18 Now all things are of God, who has reconciled us to Himself through Jesus Christ, and has given us the ministry of reconciliation, 19 that is, that God was in Christ reconciling the world to Himself, not imputing their trespasses to them, and has committed to us the word of reconciliation.21 For He made Him who knew no sin to be sin for us, that we might become the righteousness of God in Him.*

We could go on presenting scriptures that validates and repeatedly demonstrate God's continuously desires relationship with believers. We must learn to appropriate the fact that God has called us to live for Him. This kind of faith chooses to believe God's word above the evidence of the human senses. Faith in God's Word is believing God's testimony and living in agreement with it. God has repeatedly said in the New Testament that He – God, would dwell with us, walk among us. Yes, He has vowed that He would never abandon od forsake us. Through covenant, God has defined relationship as a dominate attribute of His love and purpose for us. The Apostle Paul says it clearly: *"I will dwell in them and walk among them. I will be their God, and they shall be My people"* ***(2 Corinthians 6:16).***

I cannot end this section on God's desire for relationship with us without sharing what I gleaned from the book of Exodus while in the Senior Sunday School class at True Gospel Tabernacle (smiles). The first principles I learned from the class teaching were:

1. God blesses those who accept and remain in a covenant relationship with Him. It remains true through today – He will be your God as you become and remain His holy people.
2. The second principle I was taught from the book of Exodus was simple, yet, profound – God provides and explains in great detail, what is acceptable to Him; and what is required of each of His children. God does so through His Word, His Spirit, and His chosen servants.
3. Finally, Exodus teaches us that God will respond to and deliver those who find themselves in

bondage. Understand that His deliverance is based upon your obedience and faith in God's will, which is expressed in His Word.

Today, as I look back to my Sunday School studies in Deuteronomy, I am so convicted with God's passionate challenge of our choice. Because it is by choice that we are offered this blessed and abundant privilege of covenant relationship. **Deuteronomy 30:19**, presents the dispensational conditions and choices of obedience and loyalty toward our relationship with God: "*...I have set before you life and death, blessing and cursing; therefore, choose life, that both you and your descendants may live;*"

III. God Wants to Be Understood

Yes, God wants His children to have revelation and understanding of His character and spiritual nature. **Romans 1:19-20** clearly attest to this fact. Apostle Paul declares: *"For since the creation of the world His invisible attributes are clearly seen, being understood by the things that are made, even His eternal power and Godhead, so that they are without excuse."*

Beloved of God, He wants you to search for Him as you would for hidden treasures. Look for Him in the midst of all your circumstances! Don't allow your circumstances to obscure your view of God. Sometimes, the Lord will display His presence in grand and glorious ways. At other times He will show Himself in simple, humble ways that make sense only to you. For example, in my second year of graduate school, I felt lead of the Holy Spirit to give a small local church ministry the entire amount of money I had received from scholarships and student grant monies. I told no one – only God and I knew that I had given this money to this ministry. The ministry was in great need to feed and house local families. The strange thing about this incident was that the scholarship and grant monies were never put into my hands. It went directly to the University of Illinois, Office of the Registrar. I, of course, was not allowed to withdraw any of these funds for personal use. However, in this case I felt a surge of radical faith and said within myself: "If the Registrar's office releases this money to me, it will mean that God has intervened to allow this. When I arrived at the office, an assistant said there was no way I could take money from my student account. However, as I was about to leave, a young man called me back and handed me a form. He said if I filled out the form, they would see what could be done. The form asked the "why" and "what" concerning the withdrawal and I wrote: "The Lord has need of this money for homeless persons. I believe that He will give it back to me." Amazingly, within thirty minutes or so, I was handed the paperwork and sent to the University Bank to withdraw the cash! I rejoiced that it had actually happened!

Twenty-eight days later was my registration due date for the fall semester. I was overwhelmed because I DID NOT have the money for registration. No special check in the mail – nothing! I will never forget the sound in Dad's voice when I called to tell him what I had been led of the Holy Spirit to do. Dad listened quietly as I gave him full details, then he said, "If this is truly God's doings, he will put the money back into your account. If he doesn't, I will come and bring you back home to Indiana." I was devastated!

Two days after the call to Dad, I got in the line to register, along with thousands of other students. I silently prayed throughout the several hours of the "line" process that God would not *"put me to shame."* I do recall citing my favorite **Psalms (27, 46 and 91)**. At the time, the University of Illinois had (still does) the top computer system for registration which was named "Herbie." Once your number was put in the system, it printed your financial status. At the counter, I began to tearfully explain that my account was in default; but the assistant simply snatched my form and placed it into the computer. I looked up and the huge sign said, "Herbi – makes no mistakes." I was quickly handed my print-out and it read, "Paid In Full." Amazed and believing, yet not sure I asked, "Could there be a mistake...?" The young man said, "Miss, read the sign." I softly said, "Sir, I read it," and ran out the door rejoicing.

WOW! Jesus did it! I looked at the office print-out and saw the date of my payment was the same as the date that I withdrew the money. I called my dad and he rejoiced with me. His comment? "Now you know that God talks with you." What a great day!

Now, I encourage you to ask the Lord God to open your eyes and heart to discern all of His communications to you. You don't want to miss any of the ways and things that God is saying to you. Jeremiah tells us plainly: "*And you will seek Me and find Me, when you search for Me with all your heart*" ***(Jeremiah 29:3)***. My experiences and testimonies have taught me that God's ways are not our ways, but He wants you to understand that He knows about every detail of our lives. Yes, He even knows every one of our troubles. I love the scripture that says, "*You number my wanderings; Put my tears into your bottle; Are they not in Your book?*" ***(Psalm 56:8)***. So, you must hold on and find confidence in this: "*When I cry out to You, Then my enemies will turn back; This I know, because God is for me*" ***(Psalm 56:9)***.

Yes, beloved of God – He is for you! He does not hide His will from you. Depend on His Spirit and His Word to give you a God-perspective and you will participate as He navigates His will in your life.

Lesson Three

Identity Theft

"Because the foolishness of God is wiser than men, and the weakness of God is stronger than men ***(I Corinthians 1:25).***

Over the past thirty years, I have observed a scheme or pattern which the devil uses to hinder the divine will of God in born-again believer's lives. It is quite observable, and it infuriates me to see it happen so frequently and seemingly, massively among believers. I call it "Identity Theft."

Remember, Jesus told us that the *"thief comes only to steal and kill and destroy..."****(John 10:10).*** Later in the scriptures the Apostle Paul points out to us that ... "*Satan, with all power, signs, and lying wonders, 10 and with all unrighteous deception..."***(2 Thessalonians 2:9-10)**. I have found myself rushing to the passage in **Luke 22:31-32**, where Jesus reminds **Peter** that ....31 "Satan has asked for you, that he may sift you as wheat." However, Jesus, affirms His position and declares, 32 "But I have prayed for you, that your faith should not fail; and when you have returned to Me, strengthen your brethren." Clearly, the devil desires to steal our strength in Christ, and rob us of our spiritual identity. Once you no longer live by your spiritual connection and righteousness in Christ Jesus; you are then left to live by your flesh. **Romans chapter 8** explains clearly that our life through the Spirit (Holy Ghost) is the key to our life in Christ and eternal identity! Let us look at the key principles here:

1. **The carnal mind is enmity against God!** *7 Because the carnal mind is enmity against God; for it is not subject to the law of God, nor indeed can be. 8 So then, those who are in the flesh cannot please God.*

   .

2. **Your identity is not in the flesh.** *9 But you are not in the flesh but in the Spirit, if indeed the Spirit of God dwells in you. Now if anyone does not have the Spirit of Christ, he is not His. 10 And if Christ is in you, the body is dead because of sin, but the Spirit is life because of righteousness.*

3. **You have identity and relationship with God through the Spirit.** *11 But if the Spirit of Him who raised Jesus from the dead dwells in you, He who raised Christ from the dead will also give life to your mortal bodies through His Spirit who dwells in you. 14 For as many as are led by the Spirit of God, these are the sons of God."*

Wow! Paul is clearly providing encouragement for us not to live according to our flesh, but to be "led by the Spirit." Yes, the Spirit-filled believer's identity is fully, fulfilled through our life in Christ Jesus – by the Holy Ghost!

It is imperative that we remain united by faith through the Spirit and do not lose or weaken our life which is now in Christ. We must daily know and speak as Paul said: "*...and the life which I now live in the flesh I live by faith in the Son of God, who loved me and gave Himself for me. and the life which I now live in the flesh I live by faith in the Son of God, who loved me and gave Himself for me. and the life which I now live in the flesh I live by faith in the Son of God, who loved me and gave Himself for me"* ***(Galatians 2:20).***

Beloved of God, there are many devices of culture which the devil uses today to rob (for he is a thief) believers of their true righteous identity. Let us look at four areas that can help you be more aware and decerning of the enemy's intentions to "sift" you. These four areas are not exhaustive, but I know that the knowledge of them will help you to stand stable in your Christ-centered identity.

A World of Two Kingdoms

We live in a world with two kingdoms. One is the Satanic Kingdom of darkness and lies. The other is the Kingdom of God's truth and love. Understand that those who live in sin are being controlled by satanic power that rules that, Kingdom. Although they might be considered moral or good people (choose a decent lifestyle), they are living in the Kingdom of darkness, which is opposed to the Kingdom of God! That is why Jesus told His followers, *"The field is the world, the good seeds are the sons of the kingdom, but the tares are the sons of the wicked one. The field is the world, the good seeds are the sons of the kingdom, but the tares are the sons of the wicked one"* ***(Matthew 13:38).***

Jesus came down to earth and declares, *"the Kingdom of Heaven is at hand"* ***(Matthew 4:11).*** Yes, the Kingdom of Heaven has come down to earth through Jesus' redemptive work on the cross and His Kingdom is given to all those who received it. The Bible explains this when it says, *"For God did not send His Son into the world to condemn the world, but that the world through Him might be saved "* ***(John 3:17).*** Standing in Pilate's court, Jesus declares, "*...My Kingdom is not of this world..."* ***(Matthew 18:36).***

When Adam chose to disobey God (sin) he removed mankind from the government of Heaven. That is one of the realities that the fall of man ushered into the earth. A kingdom of darkness that separated man from the Kingdom of God. That is why today, Agnostics say it is impossible to know whether God exist. Atheists claim that God is an invention of the human mind; and Evolutionary thinkers maintain that God is not necessary. But thanks be unto God, that through life in the Spirit, we that are of the Kingdom of Heaven can join with the Apostle Paul and rejoicingly say, *"For in Him we live and move and have our being, as also some of your own poets have said, 'For we are also His offspring'"* ***(Acts 17:28).*** Certainly, we give *"giving thanks to the Father who has qualified us to be partakers of the inheritance of the saints in the light. 13 He has delivered us from the power of darkness and conveyed us into the kingdom* *of the Son of His love," **(Colossians 1:12-13).*** For this we raise a hallelujah!

Superficial Religion

In the fall of 2022, I taught a course in the School of Ministry entitled, "Church History – From Acts to Present Day." The students and I struggled with the overwhelming evidence that the knowledge of God and true biblical Christianity, which Paul brought to Greece and Rome, was soon corrupted with a mixture of pagan, religious ideas. Historians give evidence to the fact that the form of Christianity that developed in Europe and later spread to America, and the rest of the world was greatly influenced by pagan philosophy and perverted Gnostic ideas.

And how did this happen? It happened because theologians and religious leaders tried to explain the nature and word of God through reasoning and speculation instead of teaching what God had revealed about Himself in the Holy Scriptures.

Oh my God! We looked through centuries of perverted discussions and debates of theologians who turned the knowledge of God and the power of the cross into abstract ideas that altered the scriptures and turned the truth into images and concepts of men. The Apostle Paul says it far better than I can. Look at what God says to the church at Rome:

"18 For the wrath of God is revealed from heaven against all ungodliness and unrighteousness of men, who suppress the

truth in unrighteousness, 19 because what may be known of God is manifest in them, for God has shown it to them. 20 For since the creation of the world His invisible attributes are clearly seen, being understood by the things that are made, even His eternal power and Godhead, so that they are without excuse, 21 because, although they knew God, they did not glorify Him as God, nor were thankful, but became futile in their thoughts, and their foolish hearts were darkened. 22 Professing to be wise, they became fools, 23 and changed the glory of the incorruptible God into an image made like corruptible man and birds and four-footed animals and creeping things" ***(Romans 1:18-23).*** A good deal of the confusion and conflict in our culture is because many of our leaders have never heard or have forgotten, or perhaps rejected the spiritual truth about the true God! We must become as explicit as the Apostle Paul as he told the Romans that *"the One whom you worship without knowing, Him I proclaim to you,"* ***(Acts 17:23).*** The scripture reveals this human tendency and its consequences: *"For this reason God gave them up to vile passions. For even their women exchanged the natural use for what is against nature."* ***(Romans 1:26).*** This practice has led to widespread spiritual confusion, physical immorality and social evils that attempt to invade and impact even the true born-again believers.

It is so clear! Through the choice of disobedience, man lost his identity. Through Satan's deception, man:

- Lost his revelation of God.

- Did not glorify Him as God.
- Was not thankful.
- Became futile in their thoughts; and
- Foolish hearts were darkened.

This is the true picture of "identity theft."

Seeking Wisdom Apart from God's Word.

The third method that Satan uses to steal your identity and rob you of your faith and evidence of the God life is – seeking wisdom apart from God's word! Simply put is to say – human reasoning replacing the word of God!

Seeking wisdom apart from God was used by Satan (the serpent) in the Garden of Eden. Remember, in ***Genesis 3:1:*** *"And he said to the woman, Has God indeed said, 'You shall not eat of every tree of the garden'?" Eve responded with the truth of God's command. Then the serpent said to Eve, "You will not surely die. 5 For God knows that in the day you eat of it your eyes will be opened, and you will be like God, knowing good and evil"* ***(Genesis 3:4-5)***. Of course, we know the woman collaborated with the devil while seeking knowledge and wisdom apart from her God: *"So when the woman saw that the tree was good for food, that it was pleasant to the eyes, and a tree desirable to make one wise, she took of its fruit and ate. She also gave it to her husband with her, and he ate"* ***(Genesis 3:6)***. There you have it; and two verses later she and Adam are hiding themselves from the presence of the Lord God. A true reality that occurs when we seek wisdom that is apart from the word of the Lord God!

Beloved of God, you must know and understand that human reasoning will always come to contradict the word of God! Regardless of the level of discussion and debate, the scripture is the infallible Friedrich Word of God. Over the past two centuries, the absoluteness of God's Word has come under attack by many intellectuals and some theologians from the East and the West. Names like Friedrich Nietzche, Karl Marx, Sigmond Freud, H. L. Mencken, Richard Darokins and others have presented their philosophies which question the very existence of our God. However, we know and declare what Paul says: *"For it is written: I will destroy the wisdom of the wise and bring to nothing the understanding of the prudent* ***(I Corinthians 1:19).*** You can raise a verbal hallelujah to this truth! I cannot finish this segment without voicing Apostle Paul's words to the believers in Rome:

"3 For what if some did not believe? Will their unbelief make the faithfulness of God without effect? 4 Certainly not! Indeed, let God be true but every man a liar" ***(Romans 3:3-4).***

The Power and Proof of Prayer

For me, the most powerful and dramatic key for fighting against the devil's attempts to steal my faith is the constant proof that God fulfills His promises of answered prayer! I believe that those of us who have received salvation through Jesus Christ and have experienced the power of PRAYER – experience the evidence of a real relationship with God. Yes, when you know that your prayers have been answered, the lies and doubts of the thief – Satan, are of little significance. For those of us who know that our prayers are heard by Father God – and answered, can resist, and fight off the lies and trickery of the devil. The Bible teaches the true believer the power of, and the proof that God answers prayers!

Scripture provides us with a multitude of examples of answered prayers. We see this in both the Old Testament and the New Testament. It is encouraging to know that Solomon prayed for wisdom and was given wisdom and additional blessings (see Kings 3:5-13). I remember reading Apostle Jame's account of Elijah when I was only a teen-ager and getting goosebumps! Apostle James tells us, *"17 Elijah was a man with a nature like ours, and he prayed earnestly that it would not rain; and it did not rain on the land for three years and six months. 18 And he prayed again, and the heaven gave rain, and the earth produced its fruit* ***(James 5:17-18)****.*

It is so affirming that the New Testament records many examples of God's dramatic answers to prayer! There are accounts of Jesus praying all night. Even He asked God for guidance and the strength to do the Father's will **(Luke 6:12-13)**. And remember in **Matthew 14:23-25**, Jesus had been praying before He came to the disciples walking on the water. I find myself, going to the prayer that the Lord Jesus prayed which resurrected Lazarus from the dead. This prayer always helps me cast away doubt: *"...And Jesus lifted up His eyes and said, "Father, I thank You that You have heard Me. 42 And I know that You always hear Me, but because* *of the people who are standing by I said this, that they may believe that You sent Me." 43 Now when He had said these things, He cried with a loud voice, "Lazarus, come forth!"* ***(John 11:41-43).*** WOW! The power of prayer!

Throughout the book of Acts, which records the events of the New Testament Church, you can find great faith as the Apostles and Church leaders prayed for more boldness to preach the Gospel when they were persecuted for preaching to the public: *"28 to do whatever Your hand and Your purpose determined before to be done. 29 Now, Lord, look on their threats, and grant to Your servants that with all boldness they may speak Your word,"* ***(Acts 4:28-29).*** Then, God answered their request, *"And when they had prayed, the place where they were assembled together was shaken; and they were all filled with the Holy Spirit, and they spoke the word of God with boldness"* ***(Acts 4:31).*** Now, you too, can raise a hallelujah!

Beloved of God, I see something very useful to the building of our faith through prayer as shown here in the book of Acts the fourth chapter. The Apostles recognized the need for a season of prayer that released their faith and increased the scope of their witness. Take notice of the progression of events following this prayer that resulted in a supernatural shaking. From that moment on, "mightiness" and boldness were clearly manifest:

A Supernatural Fullness – *all those that were present were again filled with the Holy Ghost* (v-31).

A Supernatural Unity – *all those who prayed "were of one heart and one soul"* (v-32).

A Supernatural Boldness – "*...and they spoke the word of God with boldness*" (v-31).

A Supernatural Submission - 33 *And with great power the apostles gave witness to the resurrection of the Lord Jesus. And great grace was upon them all. 34 Nor was there anyone among them who lacked; for all who were possessors of lands or houses sold them and brought the proceeds of the things that were sold,* (v - 33-34).

The Bible also teaches us how to pray. The disciples ask Jesus to, "*teach us how to pray*" **(Luke 11:1).** We call it the "model prayer." However, I prefer **Matthew 6:5-15**. From this model prayer provided by Jesus, we can see that prayer is sincere (earnest) conversation with God about both our needs and our concerns. Yes, prayer is one of our greatest assets for relationship with God. And your fervent prayer life is certainly a major weapon against the schemes and lies of the devil. Furthermore, we know that the Bible tells us that *God hears the prayers of the righteous* **(Psalm 34:15, 17)**. The Bible also reveals that the prayers of the "saints" are pleasing to God! **Revelation 5:8** says our prayers are *"like a sweet-smelling incense."*

Now let us not forget, Jesus instructed us to always ask:

Jesus said, *"...whatsoever things you ask in prayer, believing, you will receive"* ***(Matthew 21:22).***

Jesus said, *"So I say to you, ask and it will be given to you; seek and you will find, knock, and it will be opened to you"* ***(Luke 11:9).***

Jesus said, *"And whatever you ask in my name, that I will do, that the Father may be satisfied in the Son"* ***(John 14:13).***

Certainly, you can take courage in God's assurance of answered prayer! You are not alone. Ask God to help you. Pour out your heart to Him. He assures us that we (the believer) that He will answer when you pray! Yes, you must experience the proof of answered prayer for yourself! The devil cannot rob you of your spiritual identity when you pray. God answers prayer "yesterday, today and forever." The Bible boldly says, *"For the eyes of the Lord run to and fro throughout the whole earth, to show Himself strong on behalf of those whose heart is loyal to Him. In this you have done foolishly, therefore from now on you shall have wars"* ***(2 Chronicles 16:9).***

Now, when the devil attempts to make you feel alone or uncertain about who you belong to – tell him, "I belong to God and this is the confidence that I have in answered prayer, "*14 Now this is the confidence that we have in Him, that if we ask anything according to His will, He hears us. 15 And if we know that He hears us, whatever we ask, we know that we have the petitions that we have asked of Him"* ***(I John 5:14-15).***

Answered prayer is powerful and personal proof that your relationship with God is real! You can say, "I am who God says I am!"

Lesson Four

You're Blessed

Blessed is the man. Who walks not in the counsel of the ungodly, Nor stands in the path of sinners, Nor sits in the seat of the scornful; 2 But his delight is in the law of the Lord, And in His law he meditates day and night. 3 He shall be like a tree Planted by the rivers of water, That brings forth its fruit in its season, Whose leaf also shall not wither; And whatever he does shall prosper. (**Psalm** 1:1-3)

Blessed" is the word that begins the book of Psalms. This word is the Greek translation which means "happy." Yes, to be blessed by God is to be happy. These first three verses speak of the reward of those whose lives are distinctly separated from the world. Lives that are conducted as God's own people. The psalmist presents a picture of holy people who find delight in the Lord's instruction - His Word. Then, in verses 4 and 5 he presents the disaster and punishment of the "wicked." Clearly, this Psalm precisely speaks to the empty and unfruitful life of the ungodly: "...are like the chaff which the wind drives away." Chaff; the empty husks of grain; it has no weighty substance to stabilize it; but is easily blown by winds of adversity. While the righteous – who live by God's Word and are like fruitful trees whose "leaves never wither" and only accomplish fruit in your life. Yes, the severity of life's problems will shrink in comparison to the magnitude of God's presence and God's purpose being accomplished in your life.

Read on – and understand that the premise that this book maintains that you are:

Blessed....

Broken...; and

Given...!

Let us look at Luke's reporting of another significant event that occurred on the day of Jesus' resurrection. It is recorded in the 24th chapter of Luke. I am presenting it in the Amplified Bible, Classic Edition translation because its language describes the event so well. Mary Magdaline and the other women with her had reported to the Apostles the things which were seen and told to them at the empty tomb; Peter had run to the tomb and saw the linen cloths alone, by themselves, and went away *"wondering and marveling at what had happened."* Then, **Luke** writes starting at verses **13-35**: *13 And behold, that very day two of [the disciples] were going to a village called Emmaus, [which is] about seven miles from Jerusalem. 14 And they were talking with each other about all these things that had occurred. 15 And while they were conversing and discussing together, Jesus Himself caught up with them and was already accompanying them. 16 But their eyes were held, so that they did not recognize Him. 17 And He said to them, What is this discussion that you are exchanging (throwing back and forth) between yourselves as you walk along? And they stood still, looking sad and downcast. 18 Then* *one of them, named Cleopas, answered Him, Do you alone dwell as a stranger in Jerusalem and not know the things that have occurred there in these days? 19 And He said to them, What [kind of] things? And they said to Him, About Jesus of Nazareth, who was a Prophet mighty in work and word before God and all the people— 20 And how our chief priests and rulers gave Him up to be sentenced to death and crucified Him. 21 But we were hoping that it was He Who would redeem and set Israel free. Yes, and besides all this, it is now the third day since these things occurred. 22 And moreover, some women of our company astounded us and drove us out of our senses. They were at the tomb early [in the morning] 23 But did not find His body; and they returned saying that they had [even] seen a vision of angels, who said that He was alive! 24 So some of those [who were] with us went to the tomb and they found it just as the women had said, but Him they did not see. 25 And [Jesus] said to them, O foolish ones [sluggish in mind, dull of perception] and slow of heart to believe (adhere to and trust in and rely on) everything that the prophets have spoken! 26 Was it not necessary and] essentially fitting that the Christ (the Messiah) should suffer all these things before entering into His glory (His majesty and splendor)? 27 Then beginning with Moses and [throughout] all the Prophets, He went on explaining and interpreting to them in all the Scriptures the things concerning and referring to Himself. 28 Then they drew near the village to which they were going, and He acted as if He would go further. 29 But they urged and insisted, saying to Him, Remain with us, for it is toward evening, and the day is now far spent. So He went in to stay with them.*

Key»30 And it occurred that as He reclined at table with them, He took [a loaf of] bread and praised [God] and gave thanks and asked a blessing, and then broke it and was giving it to them.

Yes, here it is: He took the bread and asked for a blessing, and then broke it and gave it to them. Look at verse 31: *When their eyes were [instantly] opened and they [clearly] recognized Him, and He vanished (departed invisibly).*

Wow! They walked seven miles with Him and they didn't know Him! Take notice of the fact that He took time to start at the beginning with Moses and go through all the prophets, pointing out everything in the Scriptures that referred to Himself. Yes, Jesus interpreted for them the things concerning Himself in all the Scripture. And they did not know who He was!

I maintain that they ought to have known Him! The Scripture here says that their eyes could not recognize Him – "But their eyes were held, so that they did not recognize Him (verse 16). Again, I maintain that they ought to have known know Him!

By His Voice...

By His Words...

By His Countenance...

By His Spirit!

When I read this Scripture, I came alive with the revelation that He was only known to them when He sat down at the table, and He took the bread – and BLESSED IT; BROKE IT; and then GAVE IT to them. The Scripture tells us that once they recognized Him – He disappeared. Of course, once they had revelation of Jesus, they exclaimed to one another: *32 ... Were not our hearts greatly moved and burning within us while He was talking with us on the road and as He opened and explained to us [the sense of] the Scriptures? With revelation, these two disciples hurried back to Jerusalem and found the place where the eleven apostles were still hiding and gave an exciting report: 33 And rising up that very hour, they went back to Jerusalem, where they found the Eleven [apostles] gathered together and those who were with them, 34 Who said, The Lord really has risen and has appeared to Simon (Peter)! 35 Then they [themselves related [in full] what had happened on the road, and how He was known and recognized by them in the breaking of bread.*

There are several other times in the Scriptures where we see Jesus lifting the bread and blessing, breaking, and then giving – distributing it to His followers. The other event that stands out for me is at the Passover meal when Jesus sat down with the apostles as they were eating. Mark's gospel explicitly says, *"As they were eating, He took bread, blessed and broke it and gave it to them"* ***(Mark 14:22).*** Jesus took the bread and wine which were common elements during the Passover and gave new significance. He explained that *this was in light of the New Covenant* (14:27). *The bread represented His body* (14:22); *and the cup* *represented His blood that was poured out for many* (14:23-24). Today, the Church regularly celebrates this "Lord's Supper" because Jesus became our "Passover Lamb" who set us free from sin and allows us to have full relationship with God! Apostle Paul explains it clearly in ***I Corinthians 5:7, Therefore purge out the old leaven, that you may be a new lump, since you truly are unleavened. For indeed Christ, our Passover, was sacrificed for us."*** Jesus Himself speaks of the power of His redemption for us. He says in ***John 8:36 36*** *Therefore if the Son makes you free, you shall be free indeed.*

Our "New Birth" experience in and through Jesus Christ has provided us with the revelation and reality that we can live the 'abundant life' **(John 10:10)** that Jesus gives to all who place their trust in Him. Today, we sing songs that remind us that God has – blessings with your name written on them! Yes, I love singing these types of songs. Why? Because God meant every 'God-breathed' word that is written in the Scriptures to be His personal message to you. You must begin to view the Bible as a priceless treasure given by God to you! It is the only inspired, unchanging, inerrant Word of God. *"Holding fast the word of life, so that I may rejoice in the day of Christ that I have not run in vain or labored in vain"* ***(Philippians 2:16)***; So, that you experience the promise of God. God has stated in His Word that He has a plan for you; and that His plan for you includes, both, a hope, and a future. *"For I know the thoughts that I think toward you, says the Lord, thoughts of peace and not of evil, to give you a future and a hope"* ***(Jeremiah 29:11)***. God's plans are to prosper you! Yes, He is on your side, and He wants what is best for you. You are the 'beloved of God!' You – are loved of God the Creator and King of the universe. You can expect to receive an abundance of blessings. Always remember that He is the God of abundance! In January of 2023, the Holy Ghost said to me, "You will know me from now on – as the God of abundance." I began to very excited, and the Spirit said, "You have always known that my will for your life is abundance! I rejoiced and I continue to rejoice!

Read the following scriptures aloud:

"Now to Him Who, by (in consequence of) the [action of His] power that is at work within us, is able to [carry out His purpose and] do superabundantly, far over and above all that we [dare] ask or think [infinitely beyond our highest prayers, desires, thoughts, hopes, or dreams]—" ***(Ephesians 3:20 AMPC).***

"The thief does not come except to steal, and to kill, and to destroy. I have come that they may have life, and that they may have it more abundantly" ***(John 10:10)***

"You will show me the path of life; In Your presence is fullness of joy; At Your right hand are pleasures forevermore" ***(Psalm 16:11).***

"For the Lord God is a sun and shield; The Lord will give grace and glory; No good thing will He withhold from those who walk uprightly" ***(Psalm 84:11).***

"And my God shall supply all your need according to His riches in glory by Christ Jesus" ***(Philippians 4:19).***

"And God is able to make all grace abound toward you, that you, always having all sufficiency in all things, may have an abundance for every good work" ***(2 Corinthians 9:8).***

You should read these scriptures anytime you are feeling discouraged. The Word will pick you up!

I also encourage you to speak this special scripture as a part of your daily meditation. View it as the assurance that Jesus, is our Lord and 'Shepherd' who leads, guides, and blesses our daily journey through this life:

"1 The Lord is my shepherd I shall not want. 2 He makes me to lie down in green pastures; He leads me beside the still waters. 3 He restores my soul; He leads me in the paths of righteousness for His name's sake. 5 You prepare a table before me in the presence of my enemies; You anoint my head with oil; My cup runs over. 6 Surely goodness and mercy shall follow me all the days of my life; And I will dwell in the house of the Lord – Forever" ***(Psalm 23: 1-3; 5-6).***

David started out as a shepherd **(I Samuel 16:11-12; 17:15)**, so he was able to easily describe his relationship with God in shepherding terms. It is important that you too – learn to take this Psalm and build within yourself the confidence to allow God to navigate your life and have the testimony that David had. God met David's needs and He will meet all of your needs as you obey and depend on Him. The cares and struggles of this world can leave us exhausted, but Jesu, our 'Good Shepherd' allows 'goodness and mercy' to be our companions. Now, isn't that reassuring? Goodness and mercy will follow us all the days of our lives! Keep in mind, that, although we may experience many attacks and afflictions, David's testimony reminds that that *'the Lord will deliver us out of them all'* (Psalm34:19). In this 'End-Time' age, it is imperative that we talk and walk in faith and obedience to God's Word!

Obedience and Faith Brings the Blessings of God

Moses gives his third and final address to the Children of Israel in Deuteronomy, chapters twenty-seven and twenty-eight. Here we find that Moses is required to address the Children of Israel in a covenant renewing ceremony. Moses addresses them and explains that obedience to God is essential to receiving God's blessings. Chapter twenty-eight opens with Moses saying: "*Now it shall come to pass, if you diligently obey the voice of the Lord your God, to observe carefully all His commandments which I command you today, that the Lord your God will set you high above all nations of the earth*" **(Deuteronomy 28:1)**. The next fourteen verses of blessings are clearly contingent upon obedience to God's voice and His ways. What stands out here is God's readiness to bless and maintain His covenant when we align with His will. It is clear that these promised blessings are for those in obedient covenant! *"And all these blessings shall come upon you and overtake you, because you obey the voice of the Lord your God"* ***(Deuteronomy 28:2)***. After reassuring them concerning God's promises, Moses gives those contingent upon obedience from ***Deuteronomy 28:3-14:***
"3 Blessed shall you be in the city, and blessed shall you be in the country. 4 Blessed shall be the fruit of your body, the pro-

duce of your ground and the increase of your herds, the increase of your cattle and the offspring of your flocks. 5 Blessed shall be your basket and your kneading bowl. 6 Blessed shall you be when you come in, and blessed shall you be when you go out. 7 The Lord will cause your enemies who rise against you to be defeated before your face; they shall come out against you one way and flee before you seven ways. 8 The Lord will command the blessing on you in your storehouses and in all to which you set your hand, and He will bless you in the land which the Lord your God is giving you. 9 The Lord will establish you as a holy people to Himself, just as He has sworn to you, if you keep the commandments of the Lord your God and walk in His ways. 10 Then all peoples of the earth shall see that you are called by the name of the Lord, and they shall be afraid of you.

11 And the Lord will grant you plenty of goods, in the fruit of your body, in the increase of your livestock, and in the produce of your ground, in the land of which the Lord swore to your fathers to give you. 12 The Lord will open to you His good treasure, the heavens, to give the rain to your land in its season, and to bless all the work of your hand. You shall lend to many nations, but you shall not borrow. 13 And the Lord will make you the head and not the tail; you shall be above only, and not be beneath, if you heed the commandments of the Lord your God, which I command you today, and are careful to observe them. 14 So you shall not turn aside from any of the words which I command you this day, to the right or the left, to go after other gods to serve them."

Please take notice that I have emphasized the condition which God requires of us in order to receive these wonderful blessings. The conditional requirement is – obedience to His voice, His Word, His way. Deuteronomy tells us clearly that one must align himself with this fundamental principle of 'covenant relationship,' in order to be in position to receive these blessings. It is imperative that we are taught and understand (just as Old Testament Israel) that He is a covenant making God. He keeps His promises and cannot lie. *"God is not a man, that He should lie, nor a son of man, that He should repent. Has He said, and will He not do? Or has He spoken, and will He not make it good?"* ***(Numbers 23:19)***. (I have always felt that this is one of the most important scriptures in the Bible.) Therefore, it is important to know that God is a covenant keeper: *"Then the Angel of the Lord came up from Gilgal in Bochim and said, I led you up from Egypt and brought you to the land which is swore to your fathers, and I said, I will never break My covenant with you"* ***(Judges 2:1).*** Now, let's look briefly at the principles of God's covenant.

Understanding Covenant and Blessing

In simplest of terms, a covenant involves an agreement or promise made between two parties (people) by which they swear allegiance to one another. More specifically, biblical covenants are agreements or promises which God has established for relationship between His chosen people. In the Old Testament, God made covenant with Israel, His chosen. Jesus comes to earth to fulfill God's promises to us – God's New Testament chosen ones. Thus, covenant is a crucial, biblical agreement by which God has implemented or disclosed His plan for blessings and relationship with you!

Yes, covenant is a fundamental to the Bible's story. It can be said that the progression of biblical covenant is the primary way God has unfolded His redemptive plan. We can see how God has moved from creation to 'new creation.'**(See 2 Corinthians 5:17-18)**; from promise to fulfillment through Christ Jesus. That is why we can rejoice and be confident that we (New Testament Christians) have not been left out of God's gracious plan by disobedience. Whereby, due to Adam's disobedience, he, along with the entire human race, was plunged into a state of sin, death, and condemnation. But God, through His sovereign grace did not leave us in this condition. But graciously offered to all sinners, abundant life, and salvation through the 'last Adam,' the Lord Jesus Christ with all covenant blessings! *"Blessed be the God and Father of our Lord Jesus Christ, who has blessed us with every spiritual blessing in the heavenly places in Christ" **(Ephesians 1:3)**.* The Apostle Paul also states this clearly in ***Romans 4:14-19:*** *"14 Nevertheless death reigned from Adam to Moses, even over those who had not sinned according to the likeness of the transgression of Adam, who is a type of Him who was to come. 15 But the free gift is not like the offense. For if by the one man's offense many died, much more the grace of God and the gift by the grace of the one Man, Jesus Christ, abounded to many. 16 And the gift is not like that which came through the one who sinned.*

For the judgment which came from one offense resulted in condemnation, but the free gift which came from many offenses resulted in justification. 17 For if by the one man's offense death reigned through the one, much more those who receive abundance of grace and of the gift of righteousness will reign in life through the One, Jesus Christ.) 18 Therefore, as through one man's offense judgment came to all men, resulting in condemnation, even so through one Man's righteous act the free gift came to all men, resulting in justification of life. 19 For as by one man's disobedience many were made sinners, so also by one Man's obedience many will be made righteous."

Yes, thank God for the grace and redemptive work of our Lord Jesus! Through the Son of God – Jesus Christ, God has shown Himself faithful and true to His promises to restore a people to Himself in covenant relationship from every tribe, nation and every tongue. Today, you and I can rejoice at the graciousness of God's faithfulness in offering us the mercies and blessings that are available to us: *"17 But the mercy of the Lord is from everlasting to everlasting on those who fear Him, and His righteousness to children's children, 8 To such as keep His covenant, and to those who remember His commandments to do them"* ***(Psalm 103:17-18).***

However, I must ask you to take notice of the fact that the scriptures that speak of God's blessings for our obedience to His Word; often point to the 'curses' that come from disobedience. I will always remember the emotional and soulful shock when I read the complete twenty-eighth chapter of Deuteronomy - (Of course this happened in my

Sunday School Senior Class) – I saw that chapter twenty-eighth is hugely imbalanced. Fourteen verses are devoted to blessings and fifty-four curses are a consequence of disobedience.

Now I will share with you what my Sunday School teacher said to me. I hope that it will give you the encouragement that I held on to from that day forward. He said to me, "If you focus on living under God's authority and according to His Word and Holy Spirit, you too can live as the 'head and not the tail,' and experience God's abundant blessings for the rest of your life." Do you know I believed that teacher! And I'll give you the scripture he wrote on the back of my Sunday School lesson:

"For the Lord God is a sun and shield; The Lord will give grace and glory; No good thing will He withhold from those who walk uprightly" ***(Psalm 84:11).***

Please know that as I left the youth program and Sunday School class and went into the 'Young Adult' class. I carried a card with another scripture that strengthen my faith: *"23 Now may the God of peace Himself sanctify you completely; and may your whole spirit, soul, and body be preserved blameless at the coming of our Lord Jesus Christ. 24 He who calls you is faithful, who also will do it"* ***(I Thessalonians 5:23-24).***

Yes, living in God's Kingdom brings blessings, but the blessings are contingent upon obedience!

Believing In the Goodness of God

"Oh, taste and see that the Lord is good; Blessed is the man who trusts in Him!" ***(Psalm 34:8)***

I absolutely love the passion which David displays in this Psalm. For me, this Psalm always leads me toward a desire to fully experience more. By the time I get to verse three – "Oh, magnify the Lord with me, and let us exalt His name together" – I am ready to make my boast in the Lord and proclaim His goodness! I know that I feel it and I don't need any assistance to declare, "Oh taste and see that the Lord is good," my faith is strengthened as I confess that "Blessed is the man who puts his trust in Him!" Even spirit-filled believers struggle with various fears which this world's experiences throw at us. This kind of environment should provoke us to reach out to God and build our faith in His abundant goodness toward us. The third verse directs us to seek the Lord: *"5 They looked to Him and were radiant, and their faces were not ashamed. 6 This poor man cried out, and the Lord heard him, and saved him out of all his troubles. 7 The angel of the Lord encamps all around those who fear Him and delivers them"* ***(Psalm 34:5-7).***

The psalmist then climaxes his proclamation of the blessings for those who trust in the goodness of the Lord, and instructs us: *"9 Oh, fear the Lord, you His saints! There is no want to those who fear Him. 10 The young lions lack and suffer hunger; But those who seek the Lord shall not lack any good thing"* ***(Psalm 34:9-10).***

All of us have learned through experiences that life, in this fallen world, has a way of slapping you in the face, and as your head spins you may began to struggle with various fears. We all know that the enemy of our souls will bring anxieties that attacks and seeks to weaken our faith. The devil wants you to doubt and question the very nature and character of God. God is a good God; and His character is full of goodness toward His people! Remember, even David, when in a struggle said, *"I would have lost heart, unless I had believed that I would see the goodness of the Lord in the land of the living"* ***(Psalm 27:13).***

But please take notice that David didn't lose heart because he had faith in God's goodness! He said it clearly: 'I believed to see the goodness of the Lord!' He was not speaking of heavenly-eternal goodness. David said, "...in the land of the living!" I love it! Understand beloved of God, we could spare ourselves a lot of heartache by simply spending more time thinking and meditating on God's abundant goodness.

Take a moment and build up your faith, and allow the Word out of the first six verses of Psalm twenty-seven to help you develop a more exuberant declaration of faith in God's protection and goodness as you read ***Psalm 27:1-6:*** *"1
The Lord is my light and my salvation; Whom shall, I fear? The Lord is the strength of my life; Of whom shall I be afraid? 2
When the wicked came against me to eat up my flesh, my enemies, and foes, they stumbled and fell. 3
Though an army may encamp against me, my heart shall not fear; Though war may rise against me, in this I will be confident. 4
One thing I have desired of the Lord, that will I seek: That I may dwell in*

the house of the Lord all the days of my life, to behold the beauty of the Lord, and to inquire in His temple.

(Protection & Provision)

5 For in the time of trouble He shall hide me in His pavilion; In the secret place of His tabernacle, He shall hide me; He shall set me high upon a rock. 6 And now my head shall be lifted up above my enemies all around me; Therefore, I will offer sacrifices of joy in His tabernacle; I will sing, yes, I will sing praises to the Lord."

We must be like David and make an earnest appeal for God's guidance: *"Teach me to do Your will, for You are my God; Your Spirit is good. Lead me in the land of uprightness"* ***(Psalm 143:10).***

Some Key Scriptures for Meditating on the Goodness of God:

"8 Good and upright is the Lord; Therefore, He teaches sinners in the way. 9 The humble He guides in justice, and the humble He teaches His way" ***(Psalm 25:8-9).***

"You crown the year with Your goodness, and Your paths drip with abundance" ***(Psalm 65:11).***

"8 Oh, that men would give thanks to the Lord for His goodness, and for His wonderful works to the children of men! 9 For He satisfies the longing soul and fills the hungry soul with goodness" ***(Psalm 107:8-9).***

"For the Lord takes pleasure in His people; He will beautify the humble with salvation" ***(Psalm 149:4).***

"6 And the Lord passed before him and proclaimed, "The Lord, the Lord God, merciful and gracious, longsuffering, and abounding in goodness and truth, 7 keeping mercy for thousands, forgiving iniquity and transgression and sin, by no means clearing the guilty, visiting the iniquity of the fathers upon the children and the children's children to the third and the fourth generation" ***(Exodus 34:6-7).***

" Or do you despise the riches of His goodness, forbearance, and longsuffering, not knowing that the goodness of God leads you to repentance?" ***(Romans 2:4).***

"for the fruit of the Spirit is in all goodness, righteousness, and truth" ***(Ephesians 5:9).***

Acknowledging the goodness of God should help us mature in our faith and obedience to God. It should help us know and trust the love of God. God loves us and wants to bless us! God desires that we put Him first. Jesus said, *"But seek first the Kingdom of God and His righteousness and all these things shall be added to you"* ***(Matthew 6:33).*** As you build your faith through the Word of God and daily obedience, you will find yourself maturing in your relationship and becoming more conformed to the character and image of Jesus. Apostle John explains this process. Look at what he says in **I John 2:12-14:** *"12 I write to you, little children, because your sins are forgiven you for His name's sake. 13 I write to you, fathers, because you have known Him who is from the beginning. I write to you, young men, because you have overcome the wicked one. I write to you, little children, because you have known the Father. 14 I have* *written to you, fathers, because you have known Him who is from the beginning. I have written to you, young men, because you are strong, and the word of God abides in you, and you have overcome the wicked one."*

I encourage you reader, to want what God wants! Allow the inner working of the Holy Ghost to help you die to your unrighteous ambitions. It is time to arrive at the mature level of faith that Apostle Paul came to in his ministry. He said: *"I have been crucified with Christ; it is no longer I who live, but Christ lives in me; and the life which I now live in the flesh I live by faith in the Son of God, who loved me and gave Himself for me"* ***(Galatians 2:20).*** Trust the plan of God for your life. The goodness of God is always demonstrated for us in the path and plan He has chosen for us. We can always say – "For the Lord is good and His mercy endures forever."

God Blesses Us to Bless Others

In **Genesis 12:2**, God says to Abram (his name had not been changed to Abraham) "I will make you a great nation; I will bless you and make your name great; And you shall be a blessing." This promise to Abraham is one of the most significant passages in the Bible. Abrahams' family became a divinely appointed channel through which blessings would come to all people. This promise was actualized and formulized in the covenant in Genesis 15: 18-21:*"18 On the same day the Lord made a covenant with Abram, saying: To your descendants I have given this land, from the river of Egypt to the great river, the River Euphrates— 19 the Kenites, the Kenizzites, the Kadmonites, 20 the Hittites, the Perizzites,* *the Rephaim, 21 the Amorites, the Canaanites, the Girgashites, and the Jebusites."*

This actualized and formulized in the covenant was repeated four additional time:

Twice to Abraham –

Genesis 17:6-8 – *"6 I will make you exceedingly fruitful; and I will make nations of you, and kings shall come from you. 7 And I will establish My covenant between Me and you and your descendants after you in their generations, for an everlasting covenant, to be God to you and your descendants after you. 8 Also I give to you and your descendants after you the land in which you are a stranger, all the land of Canaan, as an everlasting possession; and I will be their God."*

Genesis 22:16-18 – *"16 and said: "By Myself I have sworn, says the Lord, because you have done this thing, and have not withheld your son, your only son— 17 blessing I will bless you, and multiplying I will multiply your descendants as the stars of the heaven and as the sand which is on the seashore; and your descendants shall possess the gate of their enemies. 18 In your seed all the nations of the earth shall be blessed, because you have obeyed My voice."*

Once to Isaac –

Genesis 26:3-4 – *"13 And behold, the Lord stood above it and said: "I am the Lord God of Abraham your father and the God of Isaac; the land on which you lie I will give to you and your descendants. 14 Also your descendants shall be as the dust of the earth; you shall spread abroad to the west and the east,* *to the north and the south; and in you and in your seed all the families of the earth shall be blessed."*

Once to Jacob –

Genesis 28:13-14 *- 13 And behold, the Lord stood above it and said: "I am the Lord God of Abraham your father and the God of Isaac; the land on which you lie I will give to you and your descendants. 14 Also your descendants shall be as the dust of the earth; you shall spread abroad to the west and the east, to the north and the south; and in you and in your seed all the families of the earth shall be blessed."*

God tells Abraham this:

#1 – I will bless you, then God says –

#2 – You will bless others. We clearly see the principle of blessings here. God gives blessings to you, and you are responsible to bless others.

"I will bless those who bless you, and I will curse him who curses you; And in you all the families of the earth shall be blessed" ***(Genesis 12:3).***

Get excited because this promise is emphasized in the New Testament. The apostle proclaims:

"6 Just as Abraham "believed God, and it was accounted to him for righteousness. 7 Therefore know that only those who are of faith are sons of Abraham" ***(Galatians 3:6-7).***

Now, God includes all of us who are saved by faith, although Gentiles, we too are included in the changeless promise of Abraham: *8 And the Scripture, foreseeing that*

God would justify the Gentiles by faith, preached the gospel to Abraham beforehand, saying, "In you all the nations shall be blessed." 9 So then those who are of faith are blessed with believing Abraham" ***(Galatians 3:8-9).***

I cannot end this discussion without pointing to our 'sonship' through Jesus Christ, and our being 'heirs' of the promise of Abraham: *"27 For as many of you as were baptized into Christ have put on Christ. 28 There is neither Jew nor Greek, there is neither slave nor free, there is neither male nor female; for you are all one in Christ Jesus. 29 And if you are Christ's, then you are Abraham's seed, and heirs according to the promise"* ***(Galatians 3:27-29).***

Yes, we were once stranger, the scripture says, *"That at that time you were without Christ, being aliens from the commonwealth of Israel and strangers from the covenants of promise, having no hope and without God in the world"* ***(Ephesians 2:12).*** Take a moment and thank God for Jesus! You and I can truly testify that we have been bought by the blood of Christ and have eternal rights to the promise and blessing of Abraham!

Giving Is the 'Measure' of Our Blessing

God is the 'God of abundance!' We know from John 10:10 that Jesus came to give us an 'abundant life.' The new life you have in Jesus Christ is to be filled with provisions and abundance. Scriptures in the Old and New Testaments assure us that He will both supply all our needs and give us resources to fulfill our God-given assignments and purpose in this life. We have already looked at many of these scriptures. Now let us look briefly at the responsibility and measure of what we are charged to do with these blessings. Jesus called His disciples to Himself and taught them. It is recorded in ***Luke 6:38****: "Give, and it will be given to you: good measure, pressed down, shaken together, and running over will be put into your bosom."*

And in the latter part of that verse is key for being a blessing to others. The guidelines for good stewardship of our blessings: *"For with the same measure that you use, it will be measured back to you"* ***(Luke 6:38).***

I was thirteen years old when I began to practice the principle of tithe and offering. I learned the passage of **Malachi 3:10**, by heart, and loved the latter part where God says *"...that there may be food in My house, and try Me now in this," says the Lord of hosts, "If I will not open for you the windows of heaven and pour out for you such blessing that there will not be room enough to receive it."*

The very thought of the Almighty God saying "prove me" always gave me goosebumps! As I became obedient in tithe and offering, I became provoked to do what Jesus said in Luke 6:38. My eyes were opened, and I clearly understood that I would be blessed in order to be a blessing to others. When I turned fourteen, my parents allowed me to have my first job – it was babysitting the neighbor's grandchild. When the baby boy would fall asleep, I would read from my Bible. I stumbled upon the passage of scripture where God appeared to Abram and said, *"...I am Almighty God; walk before Me and be blameless"* ***(Genisis 17:1)***. I asked my dad about the passage, and he explained the Hebrew translation which means "El Shaddai" or "The All-Sufficient One." I got it; it means God is more than enough! I found myself overjoyed with giving my time, resources, and all blessings. I knew that "El Shaddai" would keep His Word!

Receive, and Then – Give!

This is what I close this chapter with: Receive the blessings and promises of God in your life; then abundantly give and share with others. Clearly, we are blessed to be a blessing. One of the parables of Jesus, which has had great impact on my life is the parable of the 'Good Samaritan.' Luke's gospel introduces this parable with a certain lawyer who sought to question Jesus and test Him. So, he asked Jesus, "What shall I do to inherit eternal life?" Jesus' response was "*What is written...*" (Luke 10:27). The lawyer's reply was:

"*You shall love the Lord your God with all your heart, with all your soul, with all your strength, and with all your mind,' and 'your neighbor as yourself.*"

Jesus tells the lawyer that he has rightly answered. But the lawyer wanting to justify himself, said to Jesus, "Well, who is my neighbor?" Then, Jesus proceeds and tells the parable of a man who traveled from Jerusalem to Jericho and fell among thieves and evil men who wounded him and left him lying half-dead. A Priest and a Levite came by the dying man and did nothing. But a Samaritan came by, and when he saw the wounded man, he had compassion. The catalyst of the story is the Samaritan who bandaged the man's wounds, took him to the inn to take care of him. Before he departed on the next day, he paid the bill and said to the innkeeper, *"Take care of him; and whatever more you spend, when I come again, I will repay you"* ***(Luke 10:35)***. The exchange then climaxes with Jesus asking: "So, which of these three do you think was a neighbor to him who fell among thieves?" The lawyer of course said, *"He who showed mercy on him"* ***(Luke 10:37)***. Jesus said to him four words: "Go and do likewise."

That is our Christian assignment...BE BLESSED!

Lesson Five

Broken

"But we have this treasure in earthen vessels, that the excellence of the power may be of God and not of us." (***2 Corinthians 4:7)***

Growing up as a poor, African American kid, in a large family with sixteen children, in a "one-horse" town in southern Indiana, afforded me the opportunity to experience and learn a lot about pain and brokenness. However, I must add to that description that I had a mother who was full of devotion toward God and a father with radical – and truly dogmatic faith in the Scriptures. Especially during my childhood, I was given a strong biblical perspective on the goodness of God and the assurance *"...that all things work together for good to those who love God, to those who are the called according to His purpose."* ***(Romans 8:28)***. Even as a teenager, I found myself knowing that Spirit-filled Christians were required to endure disappointments, adversity, and even human tragedy. I can still remember hearing my Sunday School teacher say, "Never allow your spiritual life in Christ to be corrupted by the pain of your circumstances or tough situations." WOW! I believe that on that day – I gained an understanding of spiritually equilibrium through trusting the God of the Scriptures.

Please understand, I have often felt the frustrations that accompany hardships, tough situations, and the pains of human failure. However, I know that it was on that Sunday – in my Intermediate class, that God planted these scriptures in my heart: ***2 Corinthians 4:8-9*** *– 8 I speak not by commandment, but I am testing the sincerity of your love by the diligence of others. 9 For you know the grace of our Lord Jesus Christ, that though He was rich, yet for your sakes He became poor, that you through His poverty might become rich.*

2 Corinthians 4:10 *– always carrying about in the body the dying of the Lord Jesus, that the life of Jesus also may be manifested in our body.*

Philippians 1:6 *– being confident of this very thing, that He who has begun a good work in you will complete it until the day of Jesus Christ.*

Beloved, it was during my teens that I truly learned that the 8th chapter of Romans was one of the greatest chapters in the Bible for me! My strength through that chapter assured me that we are children of God **(Roman 8:16)**. I believed that God would never leave me nor forsake me, therefore, I knew that God had a purpose for every event in my life: ***"Romans 8:17-18*** *– 17 and if children, then heirs—heirs of God and joint heirs with Christ, if indeed we suffer with Him, that we may also be glorified together. 18 For I consider that the sufferings of this present time are not worthy to be compared with the glory which shall be revealed in us."*

Throughout my young adult years, I was familiar with the phase that just about every aged person would say: "God never promised anyone a life free from pain." My parents often reminded me, 'Elaine, the fact is that God does not insulate those He loves from pain and suffering.' Later in life, when I was teaching a course in World Religion at the University of Illinois, I became aware of the flawed thinking that many people have toward the issue of human suffering; especially what they view as God's position in this matter. During this time of my life, I was exposed to a great amount of flawed and non-scriptural theology. Although, I struggled with my father's view that "struggles and hardship drive us closer to God," I could observe in scripture that difficulties are a necessary component for building the foundation of our faith – those struggles and pain cause us to seek God! Certainly, those circumstances exposed my lack of self-sufficiency and convinced me to depend upon God. I still cling to the message Bible's statement from ***James 1:2-4****: Consider it a sheer gift, friends, when tests and challenges come at you from all sides. You know that under pressure, your faith-life is forced into the open and shows its true colors. So don't try to get out of anything prematurely. Let it do its work so you become mature and well-developed, not deficient in any way.*

Now, look at Paul's declaration to the Church in Galatia:

I have been crucified with Christ; it is no longer I who live, but Christ lives in me; and the life which I now live in the flesh I live by faith in the Son of God, who loved me and gave Himself for me **(Galatians 2:20)**.

So then, lets us look at Jesus, whom God allowed to suffer great pain from the cross. He also suffered the shame of the cross, and the glory! You must have the correct perspective. You know that "I walk in Christ" has taught that the presence of hardship does not imply that there is absence of God in your life! To the contrary! You can be certain that God is right there with you! God is there – wanting to reveal Himself to you. God wants you to understand that He will not leave you alone during your time of pain and brokenness. David speaks continually in the Psalms about the presence of God "in the time of trouble." Beloved, let me remind you again, that if God does not remove the pain and difficulty, but he will be there with you through it all. I still find myself singing the old Andre Crouch song:

Through it all, through it all

I've learned to trust in Jesus,

I've learned to trust in God.

Through it all, through it all

I've learned to depend upon His Word.

Beloved of God, we are "Blessed and then, Broken..." That is what God wants you to open your spiritual eyes to, and have the understanding needed to interpret how He is working in your life. Let's look closely at the segment your

Bible refers to as *"The Road to Emmaus"* ***(Luke 24:13-27)***. This event occurs on the Sunday of Jesus Christ's resurrection! Mary Magdalene and the other women have returned from the empty tomb and reported to the eleven apostles that Christ has risen. Peter hears her report and rushes to the tomb. He looks inside and sees only the linen cloths; then runs away amazed and wondering within himself at that which had come to pass. He didn't know how to interpret what had happened. He was amazed but did not understand what had occurred. The scripture then says, *"Now behold, two of them were traveling that same day to a village called Emmaus, which was seven miles from Jerusalem"* ***(Luke 24:13)***. The next 15 verses detail the conversation and significant behavior of Jesus and these disciples. It is here in this passage that Jesus reveals Himself to these two disciples. Once they get to the village, He reveals Himself through "the breaking of bread!"

Luke 24:30-35 *Then their eye were opened and they knew Him...v 31) "30 "Now it came to pass, as He sat at the table with them, that He took bread, blessed and broke it, and gave it to them. 31 Then their eyes were opened and they knew Him; and He vanished from their sight. 32 And they said to one another, "Did not our heart burn within us while He talked with us on the road, and while He opened the Scriptures to us?" 33 So they rose up that very hour and returned to Jerusalem, and found the eleven and those who were with them gathered together, 34 saying, "The Lord is risen indeed, and has appeared to Simon!" 35 And they told about the things that had happened on the road, and how He was known to them in the breaking of bread."*

I hope that you are enjoying this as much as I am! These two disciples ran back (It only takes an hour) to Jerusalem to tell the eleven what had happened. Upon their arrival Jesus appears, again!

"45 And He opened their understanding, that they might comprehend the Scriptures. 46 Then He said to them, "Thus it is written, and thus it was necessary for the Christ to suffer and to rise from the dead the third day, 47 and that repentance and remission of sins should be preached in His name to all nations, beginning at Jerusalem. 48 And you are witnesses of these things" ***(Luke 24:45-48).***

The reality of the risen Lord! Yes, He was known to them in "the breaking of the bread!" The "eyes of their understanding" were opened, and they knew Him as their resurrected Savior! At this point, I feel compelled to say to us today, who know Him as Lord and Savior; they too ought to have known Him! I propose to you four reasons why they should have known that it was Jesus, their Master:

1 They should have known Him by His voice –

John 10:4 – *"And when he brings out his own sheep, he goes before them; and the sheep follow him, for they know his voice."*

John 10:14 – *"I am the good shepherd; and I know My sheep and am known by My own."*

John 10:27 – *"My sheep hear My voice, and I know them, and they follow Me."*

2 They should have known Him by His Word –

Luke 24:25 *– "Then He said to them, "O foolish ones, and slow of heart to believe in all that the prophets have spoken! "*

Luke 24:27 *– "And beginning at Moses and all the Prophets, He expounded to them in all the Scriptures the things concerning Himself."*

Luke 24:44-45 *– "44 Then He said to them, "These are the words which I spoke to you while I was still with you, that all things must be fulfilled which were written in the Law of Moses and the Prophets and the Psalms concerning Me." 45 And He opened their understanding, that they might comprehend the Scriptures."*

3 They should have known Him by His countenance.

Luke 24:37-39 *– "37 But they were terrified and frightened, and supposed they had seen a spirit. 38 And He said to them, "Why are you troubled? And why do doubts arise in your hearts? 39 Behold My hands and My feet, that it is I, Myself. Handle Me and see, for a spirit does not have flesh and bones as you see I have."*

4 They should have known Him by His Spirit.

Luke 24:32 *– And they said to one another, "Did not our heart burn within us while He talked with us on the road, and while He opened the Scriptures to us?"*

John 10:5 *– Yet they will by no means follow a stranger, but will flee from him, for they do not know the voice of strangers."*

It is significant today, as we look at these scriptures, to remember that the two (on the road to Emmaus) allowed their unbelief to prevent them from recognizing Jesus! They had left Jerusalem on the morning of His resurrection feeling disappointed and truly depressed about what looked like a huge defeat to Jesus' followers. Jesus' death had left them heart broken. "We don't know where He is" was essentially the complaint these men made to this very Man they were looking for. How amazing and wonderful that the One they couldn't find had come to find them – AND was walking alongside them! Thank you, Jesus!

Certainly, we take notice that Jesus walked eight miles with these two disciples, and they didn't know Him until He sat at the table and blessed the bread, then, break the bread and gave it to them. Then, their eyes were opened and "they knew Him." *Today, we know that Jesus is the Son of God who is now sitting at the right hand of the Father, crowned with glory and honor. But we remind ourselves that He had to endure great suffering to get there* (v-24-26). The disciples had not understood what the Scriptures said about the Messiah. They had forgotten that when Jesus said, "*I am the good shepherd*," that He also said, *"the good shepherd gives His life for the sheep"* ***(John 10:11)***. They were expecting Jesus to redeem them from Roman rule and set them free. The cross was a devastating event for them.

Likewise, today, there are many believers who are excited about the promises and abundant blessings that the Scriptures present to us; however, too many avoid those passages that talk about the trials and pain which are a requirement in our victorious journey. I am forever thankful that I learned in Sunday School that you cannot have one without the other! My focus here is to help you focus on this truth and accept the principle that in our Christian walk with Christ – He blesses, He breaks, and He gives us to serve the Body of Christ, His chosen people!

Here are a few significant scriptures that I know will help strengthen your faith and confidence in the truth of this; God is in your suffering:

Romans 8:17 – *"and if children, then heirs—heirs of God and joint heirs with Christ, if indeed we suffer with Him, that we may also be glorified together."*

Romans 8:18 – *"For I consider that the sufferings of this present time are not worthy to be compared with the glory which shall be revealed in us."*

Romans 8:31-32 – *"31 What then shall we say to these things? If God is for us, who can be against us? 32 He who did not spare His own Son, but delivered Him up for us all, how shall He not with Him also freely give us all things?"*

It is imperative that you began to see the circumstances of your brokenness and struggle as opportunities to showcase God's glory in your life! Yes, you must do as the apostles and, "glory in your trials and tribulations." Profiting from trials! Paul writes in His Pastoral Letter to the Church at Rome: *"...but we also glory in tribulations knowing that tribulations produce perseverance: and perseverance character, and character, hope"* **(Romans 5:3-4)**. Later, Paul tells the Church at Ephesus, *"Therefore I ask that you do not lose heart at my tribulations for you, which is your glory"* **(Ephesians 3:13)**. And, again to Church at Corinth, Paul boldly proclaims, *"great is my boldness of speech toward you, great is my boasting on your behalf. I am filled with comfort. I am exceedingly joyful in all our tribulation* **(2 Corinthians 7:4).** The apostle speaks out several times encouraging believers to be patient in tribulations. To the Church at Thessalonica, Paul says, *"For, in fact, we told you before when we were with you that we would suffer tribulation, just as it happened, and you know"* **(I Thessalonians 3:4).** That scripture reminds me of the time I called my dad from my dorm room crying profusely. I remember telling him that I could not stay on campus another day. I was overwhelmed by the pressures from my classmates who wanted me to join them in their daily smoking of marijuana and liquor to handle the anxiety and mental pressure of graduate school. I can still hear the words of my dad; "God is with you, Laine, even when the going gets tough; just ask Him to help you overcome the temptation and pressure, because He is not going to remove it!" Thanks Dad...

So, reader, I urge you to find God, in what you are going through! He is there! He is not hiding, and He wants YOU to know his presence. He wants you to know His purpose in your situation! You must learn to entrust your pain and brokenness to God. Yes, learn to "cast your cares" upon Him. Beloved, He cares for you! Allow Him in turn, to reveal Himself to you in tangible ways! You must find great joy in acknowledging your lack of self-sufficiency. Find strength in your dependence upon God! You are not lost or confused. Our wise brother, King Solomon's advice is: *"Trust in the Lord with all your heart and lean not on your own understanding; 6 In all your ways acknowledge Him, and He shall direct your paths"* ***(Proverbs 3:5-6).*** With this advice you should feel like "going on" to your place of victory! And in case you are wondering if I had victory over the pressures of classmates – Praise God! I lead seven of them to life in Christ!

When we fail to acknowledge God in our brokenness and suffering, we will not understand why and how we are able to get through it. Right!! Never forget that it is only because Jesus "overcame" that we too, can and do, overcome! Jesus said: *"These things I have spoken to you, that in Me you may have peace. In the world you will have tribulation; but be of good cheer, I have overcome the world"* ***(John 16:33).*** This is why we are to rejoice when hardships and painful situations come our way. I love the Message Bible's presentation of **John 1:2-4** – and it reads: *"Consider it a sheer gift, friends, when tests and challenges come at you from all sides. You know that under pressure, your faith-life is forced into the open and shows its true colors. So don't try to get out of anything prematurely. Let it do its work so you become mature and well-developed, not deficient in any way."* OMG! I love it! Your tough struggles equip you to endure! The Apostle Paul experienced a great deal of pain and suffering while fulfilling his godly assignments on earth.

He was beaten many times, shipwrecked several times, bitten by a poisonous snake, and thrown in prison several times. In his writing in the New Testament, Paul didn't try to hide his problems; he even told his mentee, Pastor Timothy, *"Don't be ashamed of my tribulation"* ***(2 Timothy 1:8)***. Paul had a resilience toward the overwhelming trials which he endured. Find strength and take hold to the bold grit he presents in his letter to the Corinthian Church:

"If you only look at us, you might well miss the brightness. We carry this precious Message around in the unadorned clay pots of our ordinary lives. That's to prevent anyone from confusing God's incomparable power with us. As it is, there's not much chance of that. You know for yourselves that we're not much to look at. We've been surrounded and battered by troubles, but we're not demoralized; we're not sure what to do, but we know that God knows what to do; we've been spiritually terrorized, but God hasn't left our side; we've been thrown down, but we haven't broken. What they did to Jesus, they do to us—trial and torture, mockery, and murder; what Jesus did among them, he does in us—he lives! Our lives are at constant risk for Jesus' sake, which makes Jesus' life all the more evident in us. While we're going through the worst, you're getting in on the best! ***(2 Corinthians 4:8-9/Message Bible)***

Absolutely! We never give in – NEVER! The scripture tells us that we can't imagine what good things God has prepared for those who love Him **(I Corinthians 2:9)**. You are never in the dark when it comes to knowing God's gracious will for you. Jeremiah assures us that God's purpose for us is always good and gives hope for a future:

For I know the thoughts that I think toward you, says the Lord, thoughts of peace and not of evil, to give you a future and hope **(Jeremiah 29:11).**

Stand firm on the truth that God doesn't change just because your circumstances do. During times of adversity and human brokenness, commit yourself to do the will of God. Yes, this means trusting the Lord who is the *"same today, yesterday and forever!"* **(See Hebrews 13:8)** When you have truly committed to do God's will, He will lead and guide you every step of the way. There are two scriptures that I have written on the tablet of my heart! I have found that they carried me through times of pain, adversity, and brokenness:

Psalm 37:5-7 *– 5 Commit your way to the Lord, trust also in Him, and He shall bring it to pass. 6 He shall bring forth your righteousness as the light, and your justice as the noonday. 7 Rest in the Lord and wait patiently for Him; Do not fret because of him who prospers in his way, Because of the man who brings wicked schemes to pass.*

Proverbs 3:5-8 *– 5 Trust in the Lord with all your heart and lean not on your own understanding; 6 In all your ways acknowledge Him, And He shall direct your paths. 7 Do not be wise in your own eyes; Fear the Lord and depart from evil. 8 It will be health to your flesh, and strength to your bones.*

The above two scriptures reminded me of the time in my life when I was allowing the enemy to overtake my faith and fill me with fear. I had completed my doctoral studies at the University of Illinois and was somewhat overwhelmed with the thought of "What do I do now?" I was twenty-three years old and told my professors that I was ready to "change the world! When I completed my BA degree, I felt uncertain about what I wanted to do. When I completed my MS degree, I felt inspired to move forward, but now I was questioning where I fit in the academic flow of the "intellectual environment" of my world. Throughout my academic studies I had maintained a spiritual passion and balance, serving, and ministering in several local churches. I was blessed to be received as a Sunday-School Teacher, director with Youth Ministries and Coordinator of Vacation Bible School. But now, with the completion of my dissertation and doctoral studies, I found myself before God with more questions than answers. I had several professional jobs offers from universities. I even had an offer for a "White House Internship" in Communications. I had promised my mother that I would return to my hometown – Terre Haute, Indiana, and teach at Indiana State University. My mother had transitioned to eternity during my last semester at the University of Illinois, so I kept my word to her and taught at ISU for a year.

Throughout that year I was constantly aware of the Holy Ghost whispering and saying to me, "Elaine, this is not your assignment." I thank God I was surrounded by God-serving family members who allowed me to engage myself in the local church ministry events with them. However, I spent the bulk of that year with the weight of a great passion and hunger that constantly reminded me that "this is not your destination!" I felt the "cloak" of public pulpit ministry upon me, and yet the local church placed a banner over me that read: "Elaine is a woman, and we cannot allow her to be out of order in the church!" The culminating moment came when the pastor (my dad) told me that any public ministry or evangelistic aggression on my own could make me "an enemy of the cross." I submitted and turned my attention to witnessing my students and faculty members on the ISU campus.

By the end of the second semester, I received an Associate Professorship job offer from Norfolk State University. The professorship including teaching in a program by the U.S. Department of Education and NSU's Graduate Communications Department. I was assigned to assist in the development of the graduate program in Communications Studies at the University of Puerto Rico at Caguas.

In my transition to NSU, I had decided that I would give no attention or interest to public ministry. I had suppressed my soulful pain and told the Lord of my life – any call to public ministry was over! Dead! I would just do my professional vocation and live a holy life. I did not even want to talk to others nor testify about my Christian walk. I had really decided that I could not be a 'professional female Christian!' I had told myself that it would be too painful to pursue ministry and my public image would be 'an ugly woman.'

In my second two-week teaching assignment in Puerto Rico, I began to lose the ability to fall asleep. I sought medical advice and used Tylenol for a couple of days. I could immediately fall asleep, but I began to have a repetitive dream – No! A nightmare! The nightmare was my walking, then running from a huge bulldog that had a lion's head. The dog would run toward me barking violently and foaming at the mouth! In this dream I was alone. I was running with all my strength in an empty space, with nothing to grab hold to nor anything to climb upon. I would cry to God and ask, "Will you let him kill me? Do you want me to die? Show me what to do!" After three nights of this horrible nightmare, I fainted while teaching class at the university. I was taken to the emergency services and of course the doctors could find nothing medically wrong with me. They diagnosed anxiety and stress as the major issues and sent me to the hotel for two days of rest. I did not have peace about taking the prescribed drug the doctor had given me. I was terrified to be isolated in a hotel, in a foreign place with the wrong state of mind. The nurse from the hospital called me and said, "You are a spiritual woman, so am I. You are under attack and must call someone back home and get help...call them before you go to sleep...call them now!" I placed a call to Bishop Morris Golder. After telling him the dream (in detail) he replied: "Daughter, you are called of God, and you know God! This is spiritual and you know it! Don't take any more medicine. Repent for your anger and fear! Call your dad and forgive him. Then ask the Holy Ghost to give the dream again. This time ask that you be delivered and have spiritual victory over the spirit of fear."

I did exactly as Bishop Golder instructed me. Without taking any form of medicine I went to sleep, and oh my, God – deliverance came at the end of the dream! In the dream, again I was franticly running until I ran out of my shoes and clothing. I was bruised and bleeding and this time I cried out and asked God to give me a tree...or something to climb up on and get away from the dog, who was still bearing down on my heels. I looked and suddenly a tree sprang up in front of me. Desperately I ran and climbed the tree. I reached a high place in the tree and lay clinging to a huge limb. Then, I heard the voice of God speak to me: "Look down at the barking dog, Elaine." I screamed up toward the heavens: "God, I can't look at him. I'm too afraid that the dog will climb the tree to eat me." The voice of God replied and said: "Elaine, look at him." Breathless and sobbing I looked down into the huge face of the barking dog...he was toothless! Not a tooth in his mouth! Jumping down from the tree I grabbed him by his neck and said, "You toothless dog! How dare you defy me – a woman of God! Today, I have victory over you! Today, my God has delivered me from you! As I awoke, I was standing in that hotel suite with my hands raised giving praise to God for victory over the spirit of fear! Yes, I had been overweighted with fear and doubt. I thought that the religious and gender issues within the church would never be allowed to accept me – a Black woman. A woman who did not come from economic nor social royalty. Just one small person from a poor family of fifteen children. That night I became an "overcomer" and when I left Puerto Rico, I was truly a "new creation." I knew that I was called as an "ambassador for Christ" in the Kingdom of God!

Beloved of God, I returned to Virginia Beach and in the same year became the Chief Editor for TIP (This Is Pentecost) Magazine, a publication for the Pentecostal Assembles of the World, Inc.; Director of the National Bible Bowl (P.A. of W. Youth Dept.); published Biblical New Testament Study Guides for the Department of Christian Education; and became a National Evangelist and International Speaker. You see, on the night of my deliverance (in Puerto Rico) the Holy Ghost had spoken a scripture to me that remained in my mind and spirit: *"...but the people who know their God shall be strong and do great exploits..."* ***(Daniel 11:32)***.

As you already know, we cannot take our ease and sit idlily by while the world comes apart. Mankind is headed in a very bad direction. The enemies of God have intended to slow us down and push us backward through the horrible Pandemic! The world is in geopolitical turmoil and the United Sates is in political, cultural, and racial conflict that drives us toward a cultural abyss. And the consequences of such will be devastating. Therefore, today, we must not fail to proclaim the good news that Jesus has chosen and called us to live and declare Him to our broken world! Yes, and you must always keep in mind what Jesus has promised to those who are faithful to Him in this present age. I am often unctioned by this Word that Jesus spoke so plainly:

"And seeing the multitudes, He went up on a mountain, and when He was seated His disciples came to Him. 2 Then He opened His mouth and taught them, saying: 3 "Blessed are the poor in spirit, For theirs is the kingdom of heaven.
4 Blessed are those who mourn, For they shall be comforted.
5 Blessed are the meek, For they shall inherit the earth" ***(Mathew 5:1-5).***

Lesson Six

Given

"Now there was also a dispute among them, as to which of them should be considered the greatest" ***(Luke 22:24)***

I will always remember that day in Sunday School when our lesson's topic was "The Disciples Argue About Greatness." I can still hear exchange (whispers) between my classmates and myself. "Oh, this is going to be good! The disciples really had a fight?" Now, the teacher that Sunday was a substitute, and she was rather meek and timid who allowed our laughter, chatter, and excitement to dominate the first ten to fifteen minutes of class time. We were now in the Youth Class (Senior Class – ages 16-18 years) and all of us were now, born-again believers. It was so innovative to tell ourselves that perhaps the disciples were much like us – arguing and conflicting amongst themselves. Then, the teacher said, "Elaine, would you please read aloud for us the scripture focus for this lesson?" My reply was 'Yes' and I proceeded to read the King James version from ***Luke 22:24-27*** – *"24 Now there was also a dispute among them, as to which of them should be considered the greatest. 25 And He said to them, "The kings of the Gentiles exercise lordship over them, and those who exercise authority over them are called benefactors.' 26 But not so among you; on the contrary, he who is greatest among you, let him be as the younger, and he who governs as he who serves. 27 For who is greater, he who sits at the table, or he who* *serves? Is it not he who sits at the table? Yet I am among you as the One who serves."*

I stopped reading at verse 27, although the lesson text extended to verse 30. This was my moment of genuine conviction concerning the call to true spiritual servanthood! Another student, also, truly impacted with the scripture, observed I had stopped, so she finished reading for me. At this point, the teacher addressed the class with these words: "I have prayed that all of you would have a moment of conviction from today's lesson." I know I did!

Given...Servanthood.

The scripture where Jesus says, *"...the Son of Man did not come to be served, but to serve, and to give His life a ransom for many"* ***(Matthew 20:28)***, had been stressed to me by both my mom and dad, when I had received water baptism at age thirteen. I understood why my parents often reminded me that in the Kingdom of God, true greatness is measured in terms of service to others. I understood and loved reading how Jesus, Himself, provided the highest standard of service through His atoning death! However, it was while simply reading that day that my eyes toward "serving others" was transformed. It changed my whole perspective concerning, "And whoever desires to be first among you, let him be your slave." Yes, I really got it! In the dog-eat-dog world of earthly success, you are told that you can reach success and greatness by "the mighty crush the weak" or simply stepping on others. But now, I had learned in following Jesus, you reach greatness by serving others through love! The parable of the "Good Samaritan" became a favorite reading for me **(Luke 10:29-37)**.

Luke 10:29-37 *– "29 But he, wanting to justify himself, said to Jesus, "And who is my neighbor?" 30 Then Jesus answered and said: "A certain man went down from Jerusalem to Jericho, and fell among thieves, who stripped him of his clothing, wounded him, and departed, leaving him half dead. 31 Now by chance a certain priest came down that road. And when he saw him, he passed by on the other side. 32 Likewise a Levite, when he arrived at the place, came, and looked, and passed by on the other side. 33 But a certain Samaritan, as he journeyed, came where he was. And when he saw him, he had compassion. 34 So he went to him and bandaged his wounds, pouring on oil and wine; and he set him on his own animal, brought him to an inn, and took care of him. 35 On the next day, when he departed, he took out two denarii, gave them to the innkeeper, and said to him, 'Take care of him; and whatever more you spend, when I come again, I will repay you.' 36 So which of these three do you think was neighbor to him who fell among the thieves?" 37 And he said, "He who showed mercy on him." Then Jesus said to him, "Go and do likewise."*

My first public message was from that 37th verse: "...Then Jesus said to him, Go and do likewise." Beloved of God, you must understand - God's plan for you in His Kingdom is for you to be developed and transformed through your experiences of brokenness, and then be GIVEN to others as servants of God! You need only to understand and accept the process that God presents His servants. Stop trying to force God's order to fit what man's earthly, unredeemed, and unfruitful methods. You can't interpret the Lord's doings through human thinking. Jesus says it clearly to Nicodemus, *"That which is born of flesh is flesh, and that which is born of the spirit is spirit"* ***(John 3:6).*** Understand that God's Kingdom authority and the world's system are in opposition to one another. They are in constant conflict! I say like Jesus said, *"Don't marvel"* ***(John 3:7)*** at this truth. Peter explains, *"Resist him, firm in the faith, knowing that the same kind of sufferings are being experienced by your fellow believers throughout the world"* ***(I Peter 5:9/CSB).*** Peter climaxes his exhortation saying: *"The God of all grace, who called you to his eternal glory in Christ, will himself restore, establish, strengthen, and support you after you have suffered a little while"* ***(I Peter 5:10/CSB).***

Now, remember when the mother of the 'Sons of Zebedee' approached Jesus and asked Him if her two sons (James and John) could be selected to sit on His right and left hand once He established the earthly kingdom?

Matthew 20:20-23 – *"20 Then the mother of Zebedee's sons came to Him with her sons, kneeling down and asking something from Him. 21 And He said to her, "What do you wish?" She said to Him, "Grant that these two sons of mine may sit, one on Your right hand and the other on the left, in Your kingdom." 22 But Jesus answered and said, "You do not know what you ask. Are you able to drink the cup that I am about to drink, and be baptized with the baptism that I am baptized* *with?" They said to Him, "We are able." 23 So He said to them, "You will indeed drink My cup, and be baptized with the baptism that I am baptized with; but to sit on My right hand and on My left is not Mine to give, but it is for those for whom it is prepared by My Father."*

Jesus explains to her that "positions of elevation and greatness are only determined and given by God." Again, we must connect with what (was spoken) the two disciples on the Road to Emmaus and before He ascended to Heaven from Bethany. When He first met them on the road, Luke reported that He said: "…*"O foolish ones, and slow of heart to believe in all that the prophets have spoken; Ought not Christ to have suffered these things, and to enter into His glory?"* ***(Luke 24:25).***

Then, when Jesus carries them out to Bethany for His Ascension, He again states the significance of His suffering, *"45 And He opened their understanding, that they might comprehend the Scriptures. 46 Then He said to them, "Thus it is written, and thus it was necessary for the Christ to suffer and to rise from the dead the third day, 47 and that repentance and remission of sins should be preached in His name to all nations, beginning at Jerusalem. 48 And you are witnesses of these things"* ***(Luke 24:45-48).***

Clearly today, we are the born-again believers that have understanding and revelation of the scriptures. We are born-again of imperishable seed and God has brought about a spiritual transformation inside of us! What we have been through (the testing, development and trying of our faith) has truly made us a "new creation." WOW! I often say, "I don't look like what I've been through!" We all can say that. But the Apostle Paul says it best in ***2 Corinthians 5:18-20*** *"18 Now all things are of God, who has reconciled us to Himself through Jesus Christ, and has given us the ministry of reconciliation, 19 that is, that God was in Christ reconciling the world to Himself, not imputing their trespasses to them, and has committed to us the word of reconciliation. 20 Now then, we are ambassadors for Christ, as though God were pleading through us: we implore you on Christ's behalf, be reconciled to God."*

Paul says that our assignment in the Kingdom of God is ambassadorship and the ministry of reconciliation. That is our mission to this fallen world. An ambassador is officially designated to represent and speak on behalf of the country which sent him. Yes, God is making His appeal through you! He has given to us the ministry of reconciliation. That is why our relationship with Christ effects every aspect of our lives. Clearly, the scripture tells those of us already reconciled (v-17) have the commission to bring this message to others. Get excited! The CSB puts it this way: "...since God is making his appeal through us, we plead on Christ's behalf: Be reconciled to God" (v-20). Paul says our assignment to other believers is *"...as workers together with Him also plead with you not to receive the grace of God in vain" (**2 Corinthians 6:1/CSB**).* Certainly, we are "Blessed, Broken and the -Given." This is the good news! *"This was the Lord's doing; It is marvelous in our eyes!"* ***(Psalm 118:23).***

Understanding Your Ministry Gifts

I enjoyed ministering during the early 1980s because the Body of Christ was awakened to God's purpose through ministry gifts. Dr. Myles Monroe's revelation and extensive teachings on "Knowing Your Purpose" had significant impact and influence in the Apostolic, Pentecostal and Evangelical Faith churches throughout the earthly Kingdom of God! I traveled extensively during the 80s and was greatly encouraged to influence and minister to men and women who were reclaiming God's purpose, calling and ministry gifts for their lives. Throughout my international ministry I have found that saved, born-again believers were creating a "Kingdom Culture" and understanding the value of the "Church."

Although we have seen a decline in understanding and development of each individual's spiritual gifts, it is still necessary, relevant, and needed today! Remember, God is saying to us what He said to Jeremiah in the 29th chapter: "I know the thoughts and plans I have for you." We are all under spiritual assignment to use our gifts to carry out God's plans. In **Ephesians 4:11-15**, Paul clearly states: *11 And He Himself gave some to be apostles, some prophets, some evangelists, and some pastors and teachers.*

Apostle Paul continues and tells us the three-fold reason why and the divine purpose of our gifts: *12 for the equipping of the saints for the work of ministry, for the edifying of the body of Christ, Clearly, God intends that our spiritual transformation brings about spiritual maturity:*

13 till we all come to the unity of the faith and of the knowledge of the Son of God, to a perfect man, to the measure of the stature of the fullness of Christ; And – why does God want fullness of Christ for us? 14 that we should no longer be children, tossed to and fro and carried about with every wind of doctrine, by the trickery of men, in the cunning craftiness of deceitful plotting, 15 but, speaking the truth in love, may grow up in all things into Him who is the head—Christ—.Beloved of God, these gifts – given by Christ, allows us to do the work that Christ has assigned us to do. They equip us to witness to the world and bring men and women to salvation in Christ Jesus. These callings also enable born-again Christians to live a victorious life for Christ while on earth. Next, we are instructed to "take off the old man" and "put on the new man:"

"22 that you put off, concerning your former conduct, the old man which grows corrupt according to the deceitful lusts, 23 and be renewed in the spirit of your mind, 24 and that you put on the new man which was created according to God, in true righteousness and holiness" ***(Ephesians 4:22-24).***

Recently, I am more convicted than ever before, that God has saved you and equipped you for the work of ministry. We are mature in Christ and build-up the "Body of Christ." The Church will grow and mature when all the "parts" operate in unity/harmony! The scripture is clear – truth and love! Stop looking for what you already have! Get busy being and doing what you are equipped to do!

Just as the Body of Christ is made up with a variety of people of different genders, different ethnicities, nationalities, and ages, so too does God give the church a variety of spiritual gifts. The key here is diversity! Our spiritual gifts prove that God's plan produces unity diversity! Look again at what Paul says in ***I Corinthians 12:4-7)*** *"4 There are diversities of gifts, but the same Spirit. 5 There are differences of ministries, but the same Lord. 6 And there are diversities of activities, but it is the same God who works all in all. 7 But the manifestation of the Spirit is given to each one for the profit of all."*

"For the profit of all" is the conclusive truth which the apostle presents before he names the Manifestation Gifts." In verses 28-31, Paul names the five ministries of Christ and "Motivational Gifts" that God has given. Here he stresses the truth that we are all connected by the Holy Ghost and should seek the well-being of each other, "*that there should be no schism in the body, but that the members should have the same care for one another*" (v-25). Furthermore, he explains, "*And if one member suffers, all the members suffer with it; or if one member is honored, all the members rejoice with it*" (v-26). This twelfth chapter ends with Paul exhorting believers to "*earnestly desire the best gifts*" (v-31). Why? Because these gifts must benefit the cause of Jesus Christ and His divine will for the Body of Christ. In chapter thirteen, the apostle goes further to explain that all the gifts must be present in the love for Christ and not for self-gratification. In **Romans 12:4-8**, Paul addresses the manifestation and ministry gifts, strongly admonishing us to function in compassion and

with humility. He significantly declares, "*For I say through the grace given to me, to everyone who is among you, not to think more highly than he ought to think, but to think soberly, as God has dealt to each one a measure of faith*" (v-3). We would all do well to hold on to this as a plume line!

Now, I have provided you with a chart that displays the three categories of gifts. Please identify your gifts. I often use this layout when teaching and ministering. I hope that it will encourage you to see the value for service to the people of God. It is a tragedy to the Body of Christ to hide your gifts and fail to use them. It is of excellent value for you to set your priorities and goals in the will of God.

" Refer to the Table on the next page for the Three Key List of Gifts"

Three Key List of Gifts

There are three scriptural lists which are often referred to when discussing **Spiritual Gifts**. For our purposes in this section, we will look at them in this popular way.		
Manifestation Gifts	**Motivation Gifts**	**Ministry Gifts**
Holy Spirit Gifts	*Gifts of the Father*	*Gifts of Jesus*
I Corinthians 12:7-10	***Romans 12:6-8***	***Ephesians 4:7-11***
Word of Wisdom Word of Knowledge Faith Gifts of Healing Working of Miracles Prophecy Discerning of Spirits Interpretation of Tongues	Perception Serving Teaching Encouraging/Exhorter Giving Leadership Mercy Administration Compassion	Apostle Prophet Evangelist Pastor Teacher

I am thankful That I studied the scriptures and learned the purpose and use of spiritual gifts. This knowledge has given me confidence in my calling and has enabled me to withstand the lies of the devil and those whom he uses that would want me to question my spiritual calling! It is the grace and goodness of God who has allowed me to give myself in the training and equipping of His people! And I am not ashamed of the call to preach the gospel of Jesus Christ; for it is the power of God to all who believe!

A Heart After God

I will always be grateful and thankful to God for the encounter that I experienced with Him during the confirmation of my call to public ministry! I immediately began to focus my studies of scriptures and meditation on the life of David. Then, I called the late Bishop Morris E. Golder, a great preacher and Pastor I had grown up observing his biblical scholarship and anointed pulpit preaching. Before I could tell Bishop Golder that I had been called to ministry, he said to me, "Yes, daughter, you have been called to a purpose driven life that includes preaching in the Kingdom of God." I was breathless and about to start crying and he continued: "Study to show yourself approved by God to be a skillful preacher and start by giving attention to the life and call of David." I was crazy with excitement and passionate about following Bishop Golder's instructions. Two days later I called another great Apostolic leader – the late Bishop Norman L. Wagner of Youngstown, Ohio. Bishop Wagner said, "It's time for you to embrace your calling and fulfill your purpose! He continued and said, "My advice is for you to exhaustively study the four gospels and go to the Old Testament and look closely at the call and life of David." I was speechless! They had both instructed me in the same direction! WOW! I knew this was instruction from heaven; and I LOVED it! Allow me to share a couple of things that spiritually strengthened and drought order to my walk in Christ – through their advice.

Of course, it was in my Sunday School class where I learned that *"David had a heart after God's own heart"* ***(I Samuel 13:14).*** From the time of my teens, I had often wondered if I could ever measure-up to God's estimation of David. I had often asked God, "Can I have a heart that will be Pleasing to you?" The Holy Spirit would always take me to David's beginning and the setting in which we first meet David, in the Bible. Sometimes I would find myself thinking about it and concluding that David was one of the greatest heroes in the Bible and I would never have a heart like him. After all, David was very young, and hadn't he fought Goliath with only a sling? But the more I read and studied the scriptures and focused on a "heart after God," I began to understand this: the amount of time it took for David's spiritual development – It took his entire life. It was a process that was really never finished. I get it! God was always working on David.

Yes, just like us; David struggled with life's problems. He had problems with his family, his brothers were wrong about him, his father didn't even include him when the prophet Samuel, came to find the "son of Jesse" whom God had chosen. David struggled with his pride and his flesh (Bathsheba) and took another man's wife. He later implemented a plot to have the husband of Bathsheba killed in battle. We see that David was not perfect, so what is the key to God's testimony of David? Answer - He was a normal man who pushed through his struggles and truly gave God his heart. Thus, we see that through his love, repentance and heart devotion, God was able to do great things through him. Yes, we have the ability and opportunities to do the same!

Over and over again, the scripture says, "God was with David: The Psalms provide us the evidence of David's passion and love for God. He had a passion to please God. David developed a true companionship with the 'Great Shepherd' of his soul. From his youth, David sought to know, love, and serve the will of his God! It is clear to us that David was always striving to honor and please God with his life. In the book of Acts, Paul preaches at Antioch and says boldly: "And when He had removed him, (Saul) He raised up for them David as king, to whom also He gave testimony and said, *'I have found David the son of Jesse, a man after My own heart, who will do all My will'* ***(Acts 13:22).***

You too, can have a heart after God's own heart! Let this desire become an ongoing process. Allow God to take us with our many weaknesses and transform us to a vessel that brings God great glory! Remember, that doesn't happen overnight. It is a process! Remember when David was confronted with his sin, he would repent. Whatever it took, David allowed his heart's passion to turn him toward God. You too can develop a fully, committed heart toward God! Lastly, know this – *"For the eyes of the Lord run to and fro throughout the whole earth, to show Himself strong on behalf of those whose heart is loyal to Him. In this you have done foolishly, therefore from now on you shall have wars"* **(2 Chronicles 16:9).**

"But God I'm A Woman..."

(The Gender Issue)

It would be disingenuous of me to not share with you some of the painful experiences and honest convictions that I have experienced for "just being a female in ministry." I was very young when I began to minister and have a leadership role in the church. The Apostolic Pentecostal Holiness Church which I grew up in, firmly taught that Paul said, *"34 Let your women keep silent in the churches, for they are not permitted to speak; but they are to be submissive, as the law also says. 35 And if they want to learn something, let them ask their own husbands at home; for it is shameful for women to speak in church. 36 Or did the word of God come originally from you? Or was it only you that it reached"* **(I Corinthians 14:34-36).** Of course, I had read this passage at an early age and asked my father what does this scripture mean? My Dad said in a rather firm tone, "It means just what it says; women should be silent! They have no authority over their husbands and should be silent in the Church!" In a small, shriveled voice I asked, "Well, I am not a woman yet and I don't have a husband, so, does it apply to me?" You already know what his response was; essentially, he said, "Shut your mouth, drink your water, and mind your own business (Shouse 101). I was allowed to be very active in the church and was even delegated youth leadership roles and allowed to teach the Children's Class. However, I began to inwardly question the male humanism that I saw in the church culture. By the time I turned age sixteen I truly began to question God in my prayer life and ask Him: "Is this you calling me? You know that I am a female?" Then I began to search the Scriptures and seek wisdom from Bible scholars and other learned men and women in national ministry.

Clearly, I saw the potential for confusion and conflict on the issues of, "Can a woman teach and lead in the Church?" During my freshman year of college my dad advised me to contact Bishop Morris Golder and get his interpretation on the issue. Bishop Golder's advice led me to a place of confidence in my spiritual calling and required me to study the scriptures and find my answers in the Word of God! I will share an outline of my studies with you. However, I am eternally grateful to God that I learned that God does gift men and women alike – as He wills. Yes, including teaching, prophesy and other roles of leadership gifts and callings. I learned that our Sovereign God used women in relevant roles of leadership in the Old Testament, and that Jesus' earthly ministry miraculously freed women from the cultural bondage and religious strongholds. Thus, the Apostle's demonstrate the godly value and use of women in the establishment of the New Testament church. The Apostle Paul names four familiar women as he closes his letter to the church in Rome ***(Romans 16:1-8)*** *"1 I commend to you Phoebe our sister, who is a servant of the church in Cenchrea, 2 that you may receive her in the Lord in a manner worthy of the saints and assist her in whatever* *business she has need of you; for indeed she has been a helper of many and of myself also. 3 Greet Priscilla and Aquila, my fellow workers in Christ Jesus, 4 who risked their own necks for my life, to whom not only I give thanks, but also all the churches of the gentiles. 5 Likewise greet the church that is in their house. Greet my beloved Epaenetus, who is the first fruits of Achaia to Christ. 6 Greet Mary, who labored much for us. 7 Greet Andronicus and Junia, my countrymen and my fellow prisoners, who are of note among the apostles, who also were in Christ before me. 8 Greet Amplias, my beloved in the Lord."* The compassionate language he uses: "*...leave her in a manner that is worthy...*(v-2-3); *to whom not only I give thanks, but to all the churches of the Gentiles.*"

During the 1990s, I was invited to some churches to minister and found myself being pulled aside by pastors' wives who would say to me, "Do you feel comfortable doing this?" Often in shock I would reply – "My new self has been renewed in the knowledge and the image of my Creator." ***Colossians 3:10*** - *and have put on the new man who is renewed in knowledge according to the image of Him who created him.*

So many times, I had to remind myself of verse 11: *"where there is neither Greek nor Jew, circumcised nor uncircumcised, barbarian, Scythian, slave nor free, but Christ is all and in all."*

Two other scriptures I clothe myself with are:

Joel 2:28-29 - *"And it shall come to pass afterward that I will pour out My Spirit on all flesh; Your sons and* *your daughters shall prophesy, Your old men shall dream dreams, Your young men shall see visions. 29 And also on My menservants and on My maidservants, I will pour out My Spirit in those days.*

Galatians 3:28 – *"There is neither Jew nor Greek, there is neither slave nor free, there is neither male nor female; for you are all one in Christ Jesus."*

Both men and women bear the image of God, and both are needed to fully reflect the image and character of Jesus! I am so thankful that I can testify that I have been strengthened in faith and character by the hundreds of pastors and spiritual leaders throughout the country (and outside) that have received my giftings and ministry. I have been 'graced' to share with Charismatic, Evangelical, Apostolic, Pentecostal, Denominational and Roman Catholic groups. In most of my experience I have learned that for Christian ministry to flourish, both men and women are needed working side-by-side. Also, before he transitioned in May of 1996, my father called me and said that he did not want to leave his earthly ministry without affirming my calling in ministry. He further explained that his 'gender position' was only based on 'what he had been taught by his church leaders.' Believe me – it brought a great sense of spiritual unity and covering that I needed. As I think of that moment with my dad, I always call to mind the prayer which Christ Jesus prayed on the evening of His arrest in ***John 17:21-22***, *"21 that they all may be one, as You, Father, are in Me, and I in You; that they also may be one in Us, that the world may believe* *that You sent Me. 22 And the glory which You gave Me I have given them, that they may be one just as We are one."*

My prayer is that we all be focused on being transformed to the image of the Son of God! "For whom He foreknew, He also predestined."

Abide In Him, *"Abide in Me, and I in you. As the branch cannot bear fruit of itself, unless it abides in the vine, neither can you, unless you abide in Me"* ***(John 15:2).***

What fundamental and encouraging words spoken by Jesus! It is also an exciting and needful instruction. The essential meanings of the word abide, is to 'remain... reside... continue firm... a stable position' (Webster's Dictionary). Jesus presents us with a sound and simple conclusive Word. I exhort you to hold onto three of the conditions and the reward for 'abiding in Him.'

Pruning for Fruitfulness – *"Every branch in Me that does not bear fruit He (the Father) prunes that it may bare more fruit* ***(John 15:2).***

Total Dependance in Him and the Holy Spirit – *"I am the vine, you are the branches. He who abides in Me, and I in him, bears much fruit; for without Me you can do nothing"* ***(John 15:5).***

Reward for Abiding – *"If you abide in Me, and My words abide in you, you will ask what you desire, and it shall be done for you"* ***(John 15:7).***

Beloved of God, this is the appointed time of the Lord for you to go forward! Do not turn nor draw back from seeking and doing the will and work of God! I believe that Heaven is saying to you: *"Call to Me, and I will answer you, and show you great and mighty things, which you do not know"* ***(Jeremiah 33:3).***

Lesson Seven

Endure It!

I cannot tell you that relationship with Jesus means that your life will have no pain or storms. However, I cannot tell you that if you walk with Jesus and keep your eyes upon Him, and His Word in your heart, He will be your umbrella. But yes, shelter and refuge in your storms! He will guide you in His path to victory in your journey to spiritual maturity: *18 The Lord is near to those who have a broken heart And saves such as have a contrite spirit. 19 Many are the afflictions of the righteous, But the Lord delivers him out of them all.* ***(Psalm 34:18-19)***

Beloved of God, through the struggles, pain. Brokenness and disappointments, God has brought you to the place where you know that you could not have survived without His all-sufficient grace. To a place of understanding that you could not have learned His will and could not have seen His purpose any other way. (Now, take a deep breath and give Him thanks!) Take hold of God's hand and be confident that He has blessed you before and He will bless you again!

What has always stood out to me in the story of Lazarus, (John, chapter 11), is that Jesus intentionally delayed His journey to Bethany, telling His disciples that Lazarus' sickness was not the center (or focus) of the events that were to unfold. Rather, the miracle which they would soon see in Bethany would be *"for the glory of God"* ***(John 11:4).***

Beloved, that is what you must look for in your struggles and life situations – "the glory of God" that will be revealed! God does not expect us to smile every time life hands us trouble. But He does ask us to look for His presence and expect Him to always pull us out! Yes, "many are the afflictions of the righteous: but the Lord will deliver him out of them all" ***(Psalm 34:19).*** Take His hand! He is there with you now and He cares.

In this season of fulfilled, godly promises and uncommon favor, please know this: You cannot find a better friend than Jesus! He is the only one who promises to never leave you nor forsake you. He will walk with you through the process, and you will rejoice to see that you are truly BLESSED, BROKEN and GIVEN!

"...being confident of this very thing, that He who has begun a good work in you will complete it until the day of Jesus Christ;" ***(Philippians 1:6).***

About The Author

Dr. Elaine Shouse Waller

"From my childhood," Elaine often says, "I found my identity and passion in the Psalm of David – where he decrees: 'One thing have I desired of the Lord and that will I seek after; that I may dwell in the house of the Lord all the days of my life, to behold the beauty of the Lord, and to enquire in his temple'." Raised as a "P.K." (Preacher's Kid) in southern Indiana by a father and family with radical faith in God, along with all the dogma of the Pentecostal Holiness Movement, Dr. Elaine Shouse Waller learned the value of integrating her faith with the skills of advanced learning and is most proud of the Apostolic background and the wealth of godly experience it birthed in her life.

Dr. Elaine Shouse Waller resides in Virginia Beach, VA., where she and Jerome Waller, Jr. are the proud parents of one son, Jerome Waller III. She is currently the Senior

Pastor of Abundant Life Ministries. Prior to this, Dr. Waller had served at the national level for numerous Pentecostal/Apostolic organizations. During this time, she was in the birthing of three churches, and established a well-received national and international evangelistic ministry.

Elaine holds a B.S. degree from Indiana State University and a M.A. degree and Ph.D. degree from the University of Illinois. Elaine has taught at Indiana University, Indiana State University, University of Illinois, Norfolk State University and the University of Puerto Rico. She is a certified consultant to hospitals and schools - focusing on various aspects of communication and human relations.

Her academic honors include Who's Who in American Education; Outstanding Personalities of the South; and Outstanding Teacher of the Year Award-1985 from Regent University. Dr. Waller has served as Director of the Visiting Black Scholar Lecture Series at the University of Illinois; and has worked at the national level with the Pentecostal Assemblies of the World, Inc. She also served as Publishing Editor of T.I.P. (This Is Pentecost) Magazine, published by the PAW, Inc.

Dr. Waller is Founder and President of VISION Productions, Inc.-Virginia Beach, VA. VISION Productions, Inc. is a professional Film and Theater Arts production company which seeks to provide "quality-redemptive art" for secular and Christian audiences. She is Founder and President of He Brought Joy School of Ministry, and C.E.O.

of He Brought Joy Ministries Inc. He Brought Joy Ministries, Inc. is a non-denominational ministry that focuses on teaching and ministering to the needs of the body of Christ. He Brought Joy is an "equipping, developing, and training" ministry that trains leaders for Kingdom work. Dr. Waller is also Founder and Senior Consultant for Transformed Community Outreach, Inc., a faith-based 501 (c)3 program, which addresses urban minority community issues. In 2014, she established Jacob's Ladder, which is a high school Mentorship program that has partnership with the Virginia Beach Public Schools.

Elaine's convictions and commitment in influencing transformation and Kingdom building principles within the Body of Christ, has thrust her into being a well sought-after ecumenical speaker, who in her own words "desires to be like the children of Issachar which had understanding of the times, and godly knowledge of what the people of God should do."

www.ingramcontent.com/pod-product-compliance
Lightning Source LLC
LaVergne TN
LVHW050316160826
845677LV00014B/3424

* 9 7 9 8 8 9 4 8 0 4 6 3 7 *